PRESIDENTIAL POWER
How Much is Too Much?

PRESIDENTIAL POWER
How Much is Too Much?

by Robert A. Liston

McGraw-Hill Book Company
New York   St. Louis   San Francisco   Toronto

Library of Congress Catalog Card Number: 70-169021

123456789   VBVB   7987654321

To David O. Strickland and Betty

Contents

Introduction

THOMAS JEFFERSON described the American Presidency as "a splendid misery." So, in my opinion, is *writing* about the Presidency.

The splendidness of the task has attracted a multitude of political scientists, journalists, politicians, government officials, and ordinary citizens. They analyze, criticize, and generally Monday-morning-quarterback the President's decisions or absence of them, as well as his motives, personality, and general character. The result is a flood of printed material that fills library shelves and page upon page of newspapers and magazines. It is heady stuff for a mere writer.

The misery of the task stems from a simple fact that many writers have pointed out. Only one man is President at a time. No other man, not even those closest to him at a moment of critical decision, can understand or even imagine the role of the President. He has power and responsibility unique in America and perhaps in the world. It seems to me that a man who has never been there can know only misery in trying to second-guess the President. Even if he could possess all the information the President possesses, he still could not even imagine the responsibilities of the office and the awesome demand for wisdom that is placed upon the Chief Executive. Only former Presidents—at this writing, Harry S. Truman and Lyndon B. Johnson—are perhaps fully qualified to discuss a President and his actions, yet they rarely do.

It may be said that analyzing and criticizing the President is an important, even vital, function in our democracy. Yet, it seems to me that the task requires a measure of arrogance. Therefore, it is with trepidation—but, nonetheless, arrogance—that I approach the subject.

There is another reason for the misery. It is hard to find any true statement written or uttered about the Presidency. To give just one of thousands of possible examples, an eminent professor of political science writing a perceptive article in a learned publication stated not too long ago that the President is a virtual dictator in foreign affairs. There is a great deal of truth to that statement, but unfortunately, or perhaps fortunately, it is not entirely true. As we shall see, the President's power in foreign affairs is limited.

Let me set some ground rules.

First, I will not be evaluating here any occupant of the White House, former or present. One of the games political scientists play (and they admit it is a game) is ranking Presidents according to such standards as great, near great, average, lousy, or disastrous, although no one has yet been placed in the last category. It is a game that will not be played here. At this writing, Richard M. Nixon is President. I will refer to him often to illustrate various powers and problems of the Presidency, but solely in this sense.

Second, at no time will I be criticizing the conduct of the office by Nixon or any of his thirty-six predecessors. Many others have already done this.

Third, I am not going to discover or analyze changes in the sources of Presidential power and the uses he makes of them. The reading list at the end will suggest some excellent studies in this area.

Finally, I will neither justify nor deplore the extent of Presidential power. I have recorded the views of many people on whether the President should have greater or less power, but I am not expressing a personal opinion on those matters.

My task, and it leaves plenty of misery, is to report the power of the Presidency and the limitations upon that power. I have divided the book into a discussion of the war powers of the President, to which I give predominant space, and his domestic powers. This arrangement and space priority recognizes the fact that a debate is going on in Congress, universities, and the press, and among the people over the ability of the President to engage the nation in war or warlike actions without the participation of any other branch of government. In discussing Presidential war powers I have leaned heavily on new studies, reports, and speeches not yet available for the most part to the public. I believe these matters should be made widely available so that national participation in the debate can be enlarged as much as possible.

I have tried to use recent illustrations of Presidential power or the lack of it because the nature of Presidential power changes rapidly. No President does today quite what he did yesterday. Nixon's conduct of the Presidency is radically different from Lyndon Johnson's. Therefore discussions of past Presidents are not very helpful.

I have dealt only briefly with the domestic powers of the President for the simple reason that many books have been written on the subject. I have amalgamated some of the more provocative recent studies in an effort to indicate where power in Washington really lies and what the President must do to control that power. All this is considerably different from the usual school civics-book treatment.

It is extremely important, I believe, for Americans to know what the President can and cannot do in our scheme of things. We elect him as a *man*. We reach a national consensus of him as a person on the basis of the public image he projects and statements he makes. We judge him in comparison with the man who runs against him. But in office what can he *do?* What can Americans rationally expect of the man? How far can he lead us? Will he take us where we want to go? Or where we don't want to go? In short, what is his power?

I am often asked how, living abroad, I can research topical books on America and its problems. In this instance I owe it all to five people who strained the postal systems of the United States and Spain in sending me books and other materials: in New York, Marie Shaw, my editor, and her secretary, Jean Sepanski, who have inordinate affection for bookstores; in Hiram, Ohio, a senior history student at my alma mater, Hiram College, Tom Geismar, who researched many specific items with great care, and Thelma R. Bumbaugh, the college librarian, who made books of great value available to me; and in Washington, D. C., Eleanor R. Seagraves, that wonder of wonders (to make an understatement), who picked the capital clean of everything pertinent on the subject. We have never met, but Eleanor has an extraordinary capacity to grasp a subject and realize what is most useful to me.

La Felicidad
Benalmadena Costa, Spain
February, 1971

After the above was written and while this book was at the printers, "The Pentagon Papers" exploded on the American scene. These "top secret" government documents are an alleged "history" of how America became involved in the War in Vietnam. They were stolen and turned over to the *New York Times, Washington Post* and other newspapers, which printed excerpts from them. I have inserted a discussion of these papers in Chapter 4.

13

Everything else was written back in the balmy days when hardly anyone knew The Pentagon Papers existed. Keeping that fact in mind, the reader will perhaps be as amazed as I am that anyone in the nation—including leading newspaper editors—could be shocked, dismayed, or appalled by the revelations from the Department of Defense. A record of neglect, deception, usurpation, abuse of classification to conceal information—call it what you wish or all of those—was there in unclassified documents, articles, books and autobiographies for us to see, read and know. But until very recently, few of us cared, did we?

July, 1971

Part I
PRESIDENTIAL WAR POWERS

Chapter 1
Presidential War
Powers Under
Attack

MANY AMERICANS are concerned, and not a few alarmed, about the power of the President of the United States. A larger number of citizens are agitating for limitations upon Presidential power, and Congress is seeking ways to control the actions of the Chief Executive.

• • • In May, 1970, tens of thousands of university students demonstrated all over the nation against the Presidential decision to invade Cambodia in Southeast Asia. The majority of the nation's universities were closed by student strikes. An estimated 100,000 people marched in peaceful protest in Washington, D. C., against the invasion. Unable to sleep and visibly upset, President Richard M. Nixon left the White House to talk with protestors.

• • • After prolonged debate, Congress passed the

Cooper-Church resolution, which denies the President the power to send American ground forces into Cambodia without the consent of Congress. This followed earlier congressional action prohibiting the President from using combat troops in Laos and Thailand, two other Southeast Asian nations, without similar approval.

• • • In 1969, by a vote of 70 to 16, the Senate adopted the National Commitments resolution which rules, in effect, that the United States can be committed to another nation only with the approval of Congress through a treaty, statute, or joint resolution. In 1970, after the President signed an executive agreement with Spain permitting American military forces to use Spanish bases, the Senate passed a resolution stating that the agreement was in no sense a commitment to Spain on the part of the United States.

• • • In January, 1971, a Gallup poll indicated that an astonishing 73 percent of Americans would like all American combat forces pulled out of South Vietnam by December 31, 1971.

Much of the nation's concern, as these few examples indicate, centers around what are generally called "the war powers" of the President, that is, his ability single-handedly to thrust the United States into armed combat solely on the basis of his personal decision.

Since 1940, in at least seven instances, Presidents on their own initiative have used American armed forces in a manner that could have led, or did lead, to combat and casualties.

In 1940 and 1941, President Franklin D. Roosevelt ordered American ships and planes to track and fire upon German submarines while the United States was officially neutral. Some historians believe these actions might have led to war with Nazi Germany, even if the Japanese had not bombed Pearl Harbor and thus precipitated America's last formal declaration of war.

In 1950, President Harry S. Truman reacted to the North Korean invasion of South Korea by sending planes, ships, and then troops into combat. The resultant war, fought under the United Nations aegis, lasted for three years and caused the deaths of 33,629 Americans in battle and 20,617 noncombat deaths.

In 1955, President Dwight D. Eisenhower sent "advisers" to South Vietnam to help train the army of that nation. The first American battle deaths occurred in 1959. In 1964, President Lyndon B. Johnson ordered the bombing of North Vietnam in retaliation for attacks on American ships and bases. A vast buildup of American armed forces began. By January, 1971, 44,335 Americans had been killed in the longest war in the nation's history.

In 1958, President Eisenhower dispatched 14,000 American Marines to Lebanon.

In 1962, President John F. Kennedy ordered naval vessels to blockade Cuba as a means of forestalling Russian efforts to set up nuclear missiles on the Caribbean island.

In 1965, President Johnson sent American troops to the Dominican Republic in the Caribbean to protect American lives and to prevent what was believed to be a Communist conspiracy to seize control of that country.

In 1970, President Richard M. Nixon ordered American troops to enter Cambodia to seize North Vietnamese supplies and to destroy enemy bases being used in the war in Vietnam.

This list does not include the use of American troops in combat in Laos. Fighting there has long been concealed from the American public, and the origins of American involvement are far from clear. Nor does this list include many other instances when American forces might have been and almost were used in foreign combat to back up a threat. Most recent examples are the Congo in 1967, North Korea in 1968 and 1970, and Jordan in 1970.

The debate over Presidential war powers has produced moments of high drama. On July 10, 1967, the late Senator Richard B. Russell of Georgia rose in the Senate to protest a decision by President Johnson to send three Air Force transports and a small contingent of paratroopers to the Congo "to help the central government quell a rebellion." Senator Russell, as chairman of the Senate Armed Forces Committee, told a hushed Senate:

> Mr. President, I have spent most of my career here in the Senate laboring and working to try to assure that the armed strength of these United States is sufficient to defend the people of this country; but I have not spent that time and effort striving to create forces that would be sent all over the world under such circumstances as these people are going.
>
> "Oh," senators might say, "there are only about 100 of them; about 60 Air Force people and 45 paratroopers." But, Mr. President, Vietnam started out with a force not much larger than this. It can swell and it

will swell if a few of our forces are killed. We should have enough sense to keep our people out of situations like this.

Historically, Congress and the executive branch have competed for power. The political history of America can be traced in the ebb and flow of dominance of one branch or the other. Congressional actions may be viewed as an effort by the legislative branch to reassert itself in foreign affairs.

In our time, a political motivation is also apparent. President Nixon is a Republican elected as a minority President. He had only 44 percent of the vote in 1968. Congress is Democratic.

Nevertheless, there is considerable evidence that Congress is motivated by other than political considerations. The debate began in the term of President Johnson, a Democrat. There has been a nonpartisan tone to the criticism. The Senate Foreign Relations Committee has found fault with the actions of Democratic Presidents Roosevelt and Truman and, certainly Kennedy and Johnson, as well as Republicans Eisenhower and Nixon.

The greatest fuel for the debate has been provided by the Subcommittee on United States Security Agreements and Commitments Abroad of the Senate Foreign Relations Committee, organized January 23, 1969. The subcommittee has an illustrious membership. The chairman was Stuart Symington, a Missouri Democrat. A former businessman, he served in a variety of positions in the executive branch and as the first Secretary of the Air Force in 1946. He entered the Senate in 1952.

Serving with him on the subcommittee were Democrats J. W. Fulbright of Arkansas, chairman of the Foreign Relations Committee and perhaps the nation's leading critic of the war in Vietnam; John Sparkman of Alabama, former Vice-Presidential candidate; and Mike Mansfield of Montana, the Senate majority leader. Republican members were George D. Aiken of Vermont, the ranking member of his party in the Senate; and two generally liberal Republicans, John Sherman Cooper of Kentucky and Jacob K. Javits of New York.

The senators set out to discover the extent and nature of American commitments to other nations and how those commitments came about. The subcommittee and its two-man staff worked 22 months on its report, traveling to 23 countries for on-the-scene investigations, holding 37 days of hearings, listening to 48 witnesses. The full transcript of hearings and associated documents totaled 2,500 pages and dealt with American relations with 13 countries and NATO (North Atlantic Treaty Organization). On December 21, 1970, the subcommittee released a short summary of its major findings and recommendations. It is incendiary material for the debate on Presidential powers.

Following World War II, the subcommittee found, the United States started construction of a worldwide system of military bases designed to contain the advance of communism in Europe, Africa, the Near East, and Asia. In the late 1940s and early 1950s, the United States formally joined a series of alliances, such as NATO in Europe, SEATO in Southeast Asia, ANZUS in the Southwest

Pacific, and the Rio Treaty in Latin America. Many treaties were signed with individual nations.

In the 1960s [the subcommittee reported] the threat of possible Communist imperialism appeared to change from one of overt aggression to subversion and infiltration. In some areas it would appear that what was considered a communist effort was actually a rise of nationalism, expressing itself by any means possible.

In any case, so as to meet possible new challenges, the United States increased steadily its military involvements abroad. Some new facilities were added, but the main growth was in expanded military assistance and training, along with joint planning and, in some cases, joint military operations. Such activites represented an increased assurance of our commitment to countries with whom we already had formal treaties.

In addition, primarily through Executive Agreements, the Administrations of Presidents Kennedy and Johnson undertook still additional arrangements. *Many of the latter were not publicly disclosed; some were kept from most if not all members of Congress.* [Emphasis added.]

With an eagerness and a "can-do" philosophy, the United States expanded its military presence abroad to the point where it assumed, almost inadvertently and without notice, a role that has been described as the policeman of the free world.

As a result of these policies, by the mid-60s, the United States was firmly committed to more than 43 nations by treaty and agreement and had some 375 major foreign military bases and 3,000 minor military facilities spread all over the world, virtually surrounding both the Soviet Union and Communist China in support of the policy of containment. . . .

In retrospect, it is easy to assert that two things seemed probable in the wake of these policies: the United States eventually would not be able to continue bearing the financial burden of all these activities; and the Soviet Union and Communist China—both of them growing economically as well as militarily—would strive to increase their military positions as against the United States.

The subcommittee inquired into several major "problem areas" of the world, as it called them. In the Philippines a mutual defense treaty was negotiated in 1951. The treaty was ratified by the Senate. In 1954, the treaty was reaffirmed by diplomatic note. In that note, Secretary of State John Foster Dulles declared "an armed attack on the Philippines could not but be also an attack upon the military forces of the United States." Summarizing, the report stated.

In this case, as in others, neither the approval nor the consent of Congress was requested. Nor, in some respects was Congress informed until long after the fact. [Emphasis added.]

When the United States enlarged its involvement in the war in Vietnam, much was made of the sending of a Philippine battalion to join us. The subcommittee discovered this was a detachment of noncombatant engineers and that the cost of the unit was paid for by the United States. Meanwhile, the United States spent hundreds of millions of dollars flying B-52 bombers to Vietnam from bases in Guam, Okinawa, and, later, Thailand because the Filipinos banned American bombers from Clark Field in Manila for political reasons.

In Thailand, the United States paid the cost of Thai troops fighting in Vietnam. Said the subcommittee:

> This secrecy made it appear that United States policy in Vietnam had far greater support from other countries than was the case. *This was pure deception, and it is one of the worst offenses a supposedly free and democratic government can commit against its own people, because it tends to destroy that trust which is an indispensable element of self-government.* [Emphasis added.]

In Laos, the subcommittee discovered that United States military forces were being used in the conflict between the Royal Lao government and the North Vietnamese-Pathet Lao insurgent forces as early as 1965. Previously, congressional leaders had believed American activities in Laos were related solely to the War in Vietnam, in particular the bombing of the major North Vietnamese supply route, the so-called Ho Chi Minh trail, which runs in part through Laos. The subcommittee said:

> . . . Senate leaders erroneously believed that United States bombing of the trail began before bombing started in northern Laos; in fact, the reverse was true.
>
> Because various United States military programs undertaken in Laos were handled by different agencies, and, because these programs varied in the secrecy with which they were conducted, any understanding of Laos

military operations in Washington was far less than in Vientiane [the capital of Laos] where the United States Ambassador coordinated and controlled all elements of these operations. The North Vietnamese, however, along with their allies and supporters, had a clear view of all these combined United States activities.

The United States, without any treaty commitment, nevertheless is deeply involved in Laos. We provide Laos with three quarters of its foreign exchange needs plus food, AID advisers at all levels of government, public roads experts, even personnel to run the Laos public information agency. All this expense, along with direct and indirect military assistance, adds up each year to far more than the Laotian $150 million gross national product.

The subcommittee found that in South Korea a secret arrangement was made in 1966 wherein all the 140 million dollars the United States provided for new weapons for the South Korean army was used instead for oil, gas, tires, clothing, and other needs of that army. South Korea insisted on this as the price of sending South Korean troops to South Vietnam.

The 1966 agreement means, therefore, that Congress will be called upon to appropriate additional funds for new equipment for the Korean Army, despite the fact *Congress knew nothing about the agreement at the time it was made and learned about it later only with great difficulty.* [Emphasis added.]

In 1960, in return for permission to develop a communications base at Kagnew Station in Ethiopia, the United

States agreed to support a forty-thousand-man Ethiopian army. The United States expressed its "continuing interest in the security of Ethiopia and its opposition to any activities threatening the territorial integrity of Ethiopia."

The subcommittee pointed out three interesting facts about this agreement. First, the need for the communications station was doubtful. Much of its work was being done by satellite. The rest could be performed by facilities in other countries. Second, the Ethiopian army has used American weapons to fight insurgent Eritrean forces, which also pose a threat to the American communications base. The subcommittee felt this could lead to ever-growing American military involvement in that country. Third, the development of a sizeable Ethiopian army was considered a threat by the government of Somali, which borders Ethiopia. The Somalis promptly beefed up their army with war material provided by the Soviet Union. A big-power confrontation was thus created where none existed before.

The subcommittee sought to learn where the United States had tactical nuclear weapons located abroad. Executive-branch officials refused to cooperate, labeling such deployment "top secret." The subcommittee report maintained:

> The stationing of nuclear weapons in foreign countries represents a special kind of commitment between the United States and the host country. In almost every one of these countries a veil of secrecy hides the presence of such weapons. *Nowhere is this veil stronger than in the United States.* [Emphasis added.]

Most people here are unaware of the fact that United States tactical nuclear warheads have been and are stationed in countries all around the world, a pattern of deployment which results in arousing deep concern in both the Soviet Union and Communist China. . . .

The placement of these weapons abroad was undertaken at a time when relationships between the superpowers was one of inequality; when the vast preponderance of nuclear power rested with the United States. In the future, however, this situation promises to be far different, if that is not already the case.

Should the Soviet Union or Communist China seek parity in the placement of tactical nuclear weapons to the point where one of them even approached the worldwide posture which the United States has today, we could face an international crisis comparable to that of the Cuban missile crisis of 1962. The United States went to the brink of nuclear war when faced with the possibility that the Soviet Union was putting missiles in a country ninety miles from the United States. We must assume that the Soviets, as they view our placement of tactical nuclear weapons in countries far closer to their borders than Cuba is to ours, will seek to break out of the nuclear ring that has been drawn around them.

The subcommittee pointed out that the nuclear weapons continue to be deployed around the world at a time when intercontinental ballistics missiles fired from the United States make the need for such weapons doubtful.

The subcommittee believed that the simple presence of American forces in those thousands of military bases around the world created an American commitment. They cited evidence that other nations and the United

States government itself believe such commitments exist. The South Koreans insist that one division of American troops be stationed on the defensive line separating South and North Korea so that an attack on the South will also be an attack upon American troops. West Germany, despite being one of the wealthiest and most productive nations in the world, wants American troops stationed within its borders as evidence that the United States will rush to its defense in the event of an attack by the Soviet Union.

In November, 1968, General Earle Wheeler, then Chairman of the Joint Chiefs of Staff, the nation's premier military position, told the Spanish general staff in a statement cleared by both the U. S. State and Defense departments, that the presence of United States troops on Spanish soil represented a stronger security guarantee than anything written on paper.

What those troops do while stationed abroad also leads to commitment. In 1967–68, American forces joined with Spanish forces in training exercises or maneuvers. The scenario of the "war game" was that there had been an insurgent uprising in north-central Spain which the Spanish were able to contain but unable to eliminate. At a key point in the exercise, United States paratroopers were flown in from Germany and airdropped, thus assisting to defeat the insurgents. The reality of such "games" came to light in 1970–71 when Spain tried leaders of a nationalist group from the Basque provinces of north-central Spain. Similar military exercises have been held in Formosa, where American forces "pretended" to help

Chinese Nationalists invade Communist China on the mainland. Said the subcommittee:

> The political implications of United States participation in actually encouraging such an exercise are all too obvious.

All of these activities—and there were many others—which have been described in these pages led the subcommittee to conclude:

> . . . in each of these instances—and others could be cited—one secret agreement or activity led to another, until the involvement of the United States was raised to a level of magnitude far greater than that originally intended.
>
> *All of this occurred, not only without the knowledge of the American people, but even without the full knowledge of their representatives on the proper committees of Congress.* [Emphasis added.]
>
> Whether or not each of these expensive and at times clearly unnecessary adventures would have run its course if the Congress and/or the people had been informed, there would have been greater subsequent national unity, often a vital prerequisite to any truly successful outcome.

The subcommittee report has been emphasized here because it is of recent origin and because it provides chapter-and-verse substantiation of United States involvement in a mass of foreign military commitments made largely on the basis of secret actions taken by Presidents and those to whom they have delegated authority.

The issue here is not whether those commitments are wise or unwise, but rather what they say about the great extension of Presidential power. The first question to be asked is, How did it happen?

Chapter 2
The Growth of
Presidential
Powers

Addressing the Constitutional Convention in Philadelphia
in 1787, Benjamin Franklin said, "The first man at the
helm will be a good one. Nobody knows what sort may
come afterwards." Benjamin Franklin's statement is a
capsule description of the attitudes that prevailed as the
Founding Fathers grappled with one of their most difficult problems, the powers of the President.

Almost to a man (Alexander Hamilton being a notable
exception), they feared a strong executive as an invitation
to despotism. The very next sentence in Franklin's statement was the dismal prediction that "the executive will
be increasing here, as elsewhere, till it ends in monarchy."
Roger Sherman of Connecticut, another delegate to the
convention, said that "an independence of the executive
of the supreme legislature was . . . the very essence of
tyranny."

Yet, the Founding Fathers wanted a strong executive. "Make him too weak," said Gouveneur Morris, "—the legislature will usurp his power. Make him too strong —he will usurp the legislature." At least two states, North Carolina and Rhode Island, had governors so powerless that conditions approached anarchy. The chaotic situation that existed under the Articles of Confederation, which called for no executive at all, led to the convening of the Constitutional Convention in the first place.

So, wanting a strong chief executive and fearing despotism, the delegates argued long and loud over the office and its powers. In her book *Miracle at Philadelphia*, Catherine Drinker Bowen described the turmoil in these words:

No fewer than sixty ballots were needed before the method of selecting the President was decided; repeatedly, delegates fell upon it as if never before debated. Five times the Convention voted in favor of having the President appointed by Congress. Once they voted against that, once for electors chosen by the state legislators, twice against that, and then voted again and again to reconsider the whole business. . . . Equally as many separate ballots were taken on other matters concerning the executive department.

Clinton Rossiter, professor of political science at Cornell University, described in *The American Presidency* his puzzlement at trying to figure out how the convention voted for a strong Presidency:

I have followed the tortuous progress of the incipient Presidency through [James] Madison's *Notes* several times, and I am still not sure how the champions of the strong executive won their smashing victory.

Torn, wanting the best of both worlds, a powerful President and limitations on that power, the Founding Fathers, in Professor Rossiter's view, looked at the man who was chairman of the convention and designed it for him:

The President was to be a strong, dignified, nonpolitical chief of state and government. In two words, he was to be George Washington.

Franklin had said it: "The first man at the helm will be a good one. Nobody knows what sort may come afterwards."

The powers of the President, as enumerated in the Constitution, are not very impressive, certainly when compared to the long list of perogatives of Congress.

1. He is Commander in Chief of the Army and Navy of the United States, and of the militia of the several states, when called into the actual service of the United States.

2. He may require the opinion in writing of the principal officer in each of the executive departments upon any subject relating to the duties of their respective offices.

3. He shall have power to grant reprieves and pardons for offenses against the United States, except in cases of impeachment.

4. He shall have power, "by and with the Advice and Consent of the Senate" to make treaties, provided two-thirds of the senators present concur. 1620385

5. He has power to appoint ambassadors, other public ministers and consuls, judges of the Supreme Court, and all other officers of the United States, but subject to Senate approval.

6. He shall "from time to time" give Congress information on the State of the Union and recommend "to their Consideration such Measures as he shall judge necessary and expedient."

7. He may "on extraordinary Occasions" convene Congress and, in cases of disagreement between the two houses over the time of adjournment, adjourn them to such times as he thinks proper.

8. He shall receive ambassadors and other public ministers.

9. He shall "take Care" that the laws be faithfully executed.

10. He shall commission all officers of the United States.

The only other significant Presidential power in the Constitution is listed in Section 7 of Article I. The President has the right to veto laws and resolutions of Congress, but these may be passed over the Presidential veto by two-thirds of the members of Congress.

But those simple powers are misleading. It was the genius of the Founding Fathers that they drafted the Constitution in the most general terms and masked great power in seemingly innocuous terms. The first power listed is that of Commander in Chief. That may not have seemed like much in 1787, but in 1971 it is enormous. The President today has direct personal control over a military force of three-and-a-half million men and women spread over thousands of bases around the world. As Commander in Chief he controls the expenditure of 76 billion dollars, the current proposed budget for national defense. He is in direct command of weaponry so powerful that a single plane or rocket could cause more destruction than that of all previous wars combined. The President's role as Commander in Chief operates at a very high level. In day-to-day and event-to-event matters, he must depend upon the military officers under his command. This leads to events he cannot always foresee or control.

Powers 2 and 5, as listed above, put the modern President in the position of controlling no less than 2,700,000 federal civilian employees, who are also spread all over the world. He not only names "all other officers of the United States," but requires opinions of them.

His power over foreign policy is found in powers 4, 5, and 8. He is chief of state, receiving foreign ambassadors. He names American ambassadors, ministers, consuls, and other officials to foreign nations. And he makes treaties. Senate approval may be necessary, but the President chooses the men to represent the United States and negotiates the terms of the treaties.

The sixth power gives him the role of chief legislator, recommending measures to Congress for its "consideration."

Finally, power 9 enables him to execute the laws. Congress passes the laws, but it is the President who determines how they are administered. Since the deed has always had power over the word, it is obvious that Congress' powers rank second to the President's in this area.

Still, a great distance separates Presidential powers as listed in the Constitution from bombers in Laos or the buildup of the Ethiopian army. Again—how did it happen?

The single most important step in the growth of the power of the Presidency was the change in the manner of his election. The Founding Fathers labored mightily over the method of selection and begot something known as the Electoral College. It was a rather optimistic idea that the best men in the nation would get together and choose the best man to be President and the second best man to be Vice President. They knew that took care of George Washington. After that, chances are, they figured the Electoral College deliberations would turn into a dogfight so that the House of Representatives would decide. This would occur under a Constitutional provision stating that the House would elect the President in the event a candidate failed to receive a majority of the electoral votes.

The elector system worked exactly as intended twice, in the two elections of George Washington. The Electoral College is still with us today, but in a form only faintly reminiscent of that drafted in 1787. Voters cast a ballot for Presidential and Vice-Presidential candidates running as a team. In actuality, they are voting for a group of unnamed, largely unknown Electors pledged to vote for the listed candidates. Later, these electors go through an absurd formality of casting their votes and "electing" the President.

The faults and virtues of our system of electing Presidents are beyond the province of this book. Suffice it to say here that what we have is direct election of the President. What is of the utmost importance is that *the Presidential slate is the only one elected nationwide in the United States.*

Representative Wilbur Mills is chairman of the powerful House Ways and Means Committee, where all tax legislation originates. The people of the two largest states, New York and California, have not an iota of say about electing him. He comes from Kensett, a hamlet in Arkansas, and represents the smallest congressional election district in the nation. Representative Mills is known to be a thoughtful and statesmanlike man, greatly concerned about the welfare of the nation, but legally he is responsible only to a rural area in Arkansas.

As a nation, the American people can look only to the President for leadership. Only he is responsible to all the people. It may be said the Vice President is also elected nationwide, but the office has almost no powers or duties other than those the President seeks to delegate to him. John Adams, the first man to hold the office, called it "the most insignificant office that ever the invention of man contrived or his imagination conceived."

Andrew Jackson, elected in 1828, was the first man truly elected by the people and he lost no time in apprising Congress and the Supreme Court of the fact. He felt that as a popularly elected President he was responsible directly to the people who had elected him. He did not consider himself in the least subservient to Congress. In his view his election was a mandate to Congress to carry out the program which he, as President, advocated.

To a greater or lesser extent, Presidents have had that attitude ever since. They have their own electorate separate from Congress. They have power with the people which no member of Congress can approach. In time of crisis or emergency, real or invented, the people expect the President to act.

The second most powerful spur to the Presidency has been the decline in the federal system set forth by the Founding Fathers. The ultimate genius of the framers of the Constitution was the way they accommodated the sovereign states in a national government. They granted the federal government certain powers, leaving the rest to the states or the people. Moreover, they made the federal government responsible to the people—not to the states. Thus both at the state and the national levels, government was serving the people.

Starting back in 1787, the power and usefulness of the states—and their stepchildren, counties, cities, towns and other units of local government—have atrophied, while the federal government has waxed strong. More and more responsibilities have fallen under the jurisdiction of the federal government. Railways and highways cross state lines; so do the operations of large corporations. Standardization and technology have grown simultaneously with the power of the federal government. Even that staunch advocate of states' rights, Thomas Jefferson, as President used broad federal powers in the Louisiana Purchase, the establishment of the second Bank of the U. S., and the granting of protection to manufacturers.

Taxing power followed. The Sixteenth Amendment to the Constitution, ratified in 1913, premitted the federal government to tax incomes (even though they had been taxing personal and corporate incomes for sixty years prior to 1913). The national income tax is the largest and most reliable source of revenue. Some states now tax the personal incomes of their residents, but the states depend heavily on sales, property, and nuisance taxes, which are inefficient and by their very nature self-impoverishing. Sales and most nuisance taxes, for example, tax the poor and not the rich. Since the federal government has the most responsibilities and the most money, it has also garnered the most power.

State governments stubbornly witnessed the atrophy of their power because they were undemocratic. State after state was misapportioned. State legislators came from districts of grossly unequal size. One man might represent a few thousand people, another tens of thousands or even hundreds of thousands. And there was a pattern to the misapportionment. Rural, agrarian voters had far gerater representation in state legislatures than urban and suburban voters. For decades the legislatures stubbornly refused to reapportion themselves. Not until 1962, when the United States Supreme Court began a series of historic decisions, were the state legislatures forced to redistrict themselves according to the principle of "one man, one vote."

During those decades of misapportionment, the population of the United States became increasingly urbanized, while the rural-dominated state legislatures remained monumentally unresponsive to the needs of urban dwellers, a group which now composes 70 percent of the nation's population. These people came to look increasingly for the aid they needed to the federal goevrnment— and to the one man they all elected, the President.

Between roughly 1920 and 1960, the United States experienced major shifts in its population distribution. The West Coast, East Coast, and Gulf Coast grew in population, along with a few inland "islands" of population such as the Gerat Lakes area. Cities grew and burst their traditional boundaries. Greater New York City spread into New Jersey, Connecticut, and even Pennsylvania; Philadelphia into New Jersey; Chicago into Indiana; St. Louis into Illinois; Cincinnati into Kentucky. Even when these and other cities did not cross state lines, they enveloped whole counties and devoured towns and school districts.

The result was, in a sense, the Balkanization of our great cities. They became, not cities, but metropolitan areas embracing dozens, scores, hundreds of autonomous governmental and taxing units. One study showed that the New York metropolitan area consisted of 16 million people living in 1,476 separate governmental units. Los Angeles perhaps has more. And the cities look to the federal government for help in solving their problems.

Finally, America become a mobile society with 20 percent of the population on the move at any given moment. Traditional loyalties to state, county, city, or town became blurred. Only the federal government, or so it was easy to believe, could provide the help, the regulation, and the governing such a fast-moving society needed.

Providing services and protection demanded by a changed society led to a vast increase in the size and power of the federal government. In 1933, when the country was mired in the Great Depression, the national government began launching program upon program—unemployment compensation, public welfare, social security, farm subsidies, loans to businesses large and small, laws for the protection of labor unions, and regulation of nearly everything, including transportation, business, banking, stock exchanges, wildlife. The list is long for the needs of the nation were many. Government went into business, operating factories and farms. It controlled natural resources. It fought crime and criminals that cities and states were powerless to combat.

The simple words of the Founding Fathers making the President the administrator of the laws rendered unto him vast power because there were so many more laws to administer. The Federal bureaucracy grew until its 2,700,000 civilian employees affect Americans in the largest and most intimate ways. And nearly all are under the authority of the President.

Federal spending for all these thousands of programs grew. In 1971 President Nixon submitted a budget of $229.2 *billion*. That is a figure so large it is incomprehensible. It is a challenge to try to make it meaningful. But let's try. Suppose all that money were spent for loaves of bread (if enough could be baked in all the ovens on earth). Laid end to end, they would reach nearly to the sun, 93 million miles.

Concomitant with the rise of power and responsibility was the growth in mass communication. President Woodrow Wilson began to hold press conferences, meeting with journalists to make statements and answer questions. He revived the practice of making his State of the Union address to Congress in person. Radio came on the scene, then television. The President, the man elected by the people, found himself well equipped with the means to speak directly to his constituents. They could sit in their living rooms and he could address them personally, explaining his motives and purposes, demanding or beseeching their support. No other single person, be he the governor of the most powerful state, the most influential member of Congress, the most learned and respected man, could command the same attention and audience. While the ability of the President to mold public opinion in support of his policies has increased Presidential power, public opinion has generated a counter-force limiting that power.

At the same time changes came in the relative powers of the three branches of government. The Founding Fathers, as elementary civics books note, developed a tripartite system of "checks and balances" between the legislative, executive, and judicial branches. Each branch was to have its own powers and its own checks on the powers of the other two.

As the power of the Presidency grew, the influence of Congress waned. Some loss of its power was inevitable.

43

It had no one natural spokesman to rival the President. At best it had two leaders, the Speaker of the House and the majority leader in the Senate. But more often it had a clutch of leaders, and a committee can never rival in prestige and influence a strong man in the White House.

More of the loss was the result of folly. Congress, like the state legislatures, was undemocratic for decades. One congressman from Michigan represented 117,000 people, another from the same state 802,000. The rural domination of the House of Representatives was broken only by the same Supreme Court rulings that democratized the state legislatures.

Worse, Congress insisted upon (indeed, still insists upon) organizational rules that have shackled its effectiveness and responsiveness and thus its power. The seniority system renders unto the aged the powerful committee chairmanships—and the aged came from "safe" districts in the South and from northern city districts dominated by political machines. Congress itself drafted rules that vested overwhelming power over legislation in committee chairmen, leaving the elected leadership of the House and Senate, that is, the Speaker and the majority leaders, relatively powerless to control legislative action. Congress thus became the depository of the elderly and the safe, the unresponsive and leaderless. It failed to initiate action or, indeed, to act in so many matters of national importance—including even the reformation of itself—that it lost prestige.

At the same time, the Supreme Court took on an activist role. Under the influence of such men as Chief Justice Earl Warren and Justices Hugo Black, William

Douglas, and Tom Clark, the Court came to play a powerful role in government. It reached out to make far-reaching decisions in apportionment, civil rights, and criminal justice. It insisted upon the rethinking of traditional attitudes toward American institutions.

But the Court itself has no power other than public opinion, the willingness of the people to abide by its decisions. It has no armies and few administrators. It depends upon the President and the executive branch to support its rulings and to carry out its edicts. Thus, one effect of the growth in judicial power was an increase in the power of the President. As the sole elected leader of the most powerful nation on earth, one man, the President, became the most powerful single individual in the nation and, following World War II, in the world.

But what of the men who have held the office? They, too, have left a legacy. President Nixon sifts in his hands the powers garnered by Washington, Jefferson, Jackson, Polk, Lincoln, Cleveland, Theodore Roosevelt, Wilson, Franklin Roosevelt, Truman, Eisenhower, Kennedy, and Lyndon Johnson. Washington personally led troops to quell the Whiskey Rebellion. He refused to allow Congress to see communications from foreign ambassadors. Jefferson negotiated the Louisiana Purchase, Constitutional authority or no Constitutional authority. Lincoln fought the Civil War by executive decree and left it to Congress to come along afterward and ratify what he had done. During World War I, Wilson assumed as great or greater powers than Lincoln, but convinced Congress and the people to grant him the power.

The list of Presidents in the preceding paragraph is no

accident. It names the men whom most historians and political scientists consider to have been strong Presidents, men who measurably enhanced the power of the office and assumed leadership of the nation at the expense of Congress. Scholar after scholar has written in admiration of these men and with scorn or sadness or regret about the so-called weak Presidents, Monroe, Fillmore, Buchanan, Grant, Harrison, Taft, Harding, Coolidge, and Hoover.

The only contrived part of the list of strong Presidents above is the inclusion of the Presidents who served after Franklin Roosevelt. Historians consider Roosevelt and Truman to have been among the great Presidents. Eisenhower, while not weak, is not considered great. Kennedy and Johnson are too recent for any extended serious judgment to be made on them. Indeed, both may be among the most difficult Presidents in history to evaluate. But I included them all to make the point that today there is no possibility of a weak President. The powers of the office, accumulated by time, a changed society, enhanced demands and the legacy of the men who have held the office, make the weakest man a giant.

Consider Harry Truman. No man entering the office considered himself less qualified or was more reluctant or awed by the position thrust upon him by Roosevelt's death. He was a small-time machine politician, a senator, and Vice President who found himself thrust into the White House at a key moment when he was virtually uninformed of the national issues confronting him. But Harry Truman was a student of history. He had infinite respect for the office and a pronounced sense of his role in it. He worked hard, he learned, he had great courage and willingness to make decisions, and a boundless desire for greatness. And, if historians are correct, he achieved it.

But are historians correct, not just in the case of Harry Truman, but in their evaluations of all Presidents? Nothing is more fascinating in the current debate over Presidential war powers than the second thoughts scholars are having about their own judgments. Hans J. Morgenthau, political scientist at the University of Chicago and City College of New York, wrote in the *New Republic* in 1969:

> I remember how I used to implore a succession of Presidents to assert their constitutional powers against Congress as long as I disagreed with the foreign policies to which Congress appeared to be committed. Yet, when I had given up on the potential for change of the Eisenhower-Dulles foreign policies, I urged the Senate Foreign Relations Committee to establish itself as a kind of counter-Department of State. And, from 1965 onwards, I would have welcomed the influence that Congress, the Senate or, for that matter, any other agency of government could have exerted in order to change the course of American foreign policy.

Robert J. Bresler, another political scientist, wrote in the *Nation* in 1970, as follows:

> Americans, especially liberals, should be embarrassed to recall, as Richard Neustadt, author of *Presidential Power*,

has acknowledged, that they helped to create the myth which so loosely equated Presidential greatness with the exercise of war powers. . . . Great Presidents would have to be strong Presidents, and for liberals it was no more than coincidence that strong Presidents invariably became war Presidents.

Marcus Cunliffe, professor of American studies at the University of Sussex, wrote in *Commentary* in 1968:

> . . . it is worth stressing that over most of America's past the White House has been occupied not by "strong" but by "weak" Presidents. Some no doubt were truly weak: inept, timorous, petty. Others however were "weak" not out of temperamental inability but out of conviction: men who did not think it right for the Federal Government to encroach upon the States, or else for the executive to encroach upon the legislature. Some have insisted that the prime duty of the President is to act as head of state rather than as head of government or as head of a political party.

Professor Cunliffe pointed out that several of the so-called weak Presidents had a "quite clear conception of their role." Grant, whom many historians consider among the weakest of Presidents, is as good an example as any of the attitude of the President who does not aggrandize powers. Referring to the Depression of 1873, Grant said:

> It is the duty of Congress to devise the method of correcting the evils which are acknowledged to exist, and not mine.

Professor Cunliffe concluded:

The charge against the non-aggrandizing Presidents of
the 20th Century, however, is not that they failed to
take personal charge over every facet of national life. It
is that they failed to imbue the nation with a sense of
Presidential greatness. Canny, homely, well-meaning,
they did not seem and were not truly eminent. Otherwise, they were not bad Presidents according to their
lights. They do not always come off badly in a comparison with the aggrandizers.

An anecdote by Emmet Hughes in his *Ordeal of Power*
perhaps best illustrates the difference in attitudes between
the so-called weak and strong Presidents. Both Eisenhower and Kennedy admired Lincoln, but for different
reasons. Eisenhower admired Lincoln's humility and
loved to tell of Lincoln's readiness to hold General
McClellan's horse if only McClellan would bring him a
victory in the Civil War. Kennedy admired Lincoln's
mastery and enjoyed telling how Lincoln wanted to hear
his cabinet's views on the Emancipation Proclamation
but only *after* he had made his decision.

But all these are second thoughts in the wake of war,
bloodshed, and great expense stemming from Presidential
war powers. The fact remains that the leading liberal
professors have contributed to greater Presidential powers
by playing their game of ranking the Presidents. Thus
they have pushed succeeding modern Presidents to "greatness" by demanding decisiveness, energy, masterliness, and
vastly increased powers.

Direct election, diminution of the federal system, mobility, growth of national power, mass communication, loss of congressional power, the precedents of the office, and the opinions of historians have all contributed to the growth of Presidential power. But when this is equated in terms of an army in Ethiopia, bombers over Laos, and Marines rushing ashore on a Caribbean isle, we must still ask, How did it happen?

Chapter 3
Congress Neglects
its War Powers

CONGRESS was not neglected when powers over America's relations with other nations were parceled out. The Symington subcommittee gave the following list of congressional powers in this area:

> The role of the President in foreign policy is limited by the specific constitutional powers of the Congress, including not only the appropriation of funds and the Senate function of advice and consent, but also the regulation of commerce with foreign nations, the definition and punishment of offenses against the law of nations, declarations of war and interventions abroad, the raising and support of the armed forces, the making of rules and regulations for the government of those forces, and provision for the common defense and general welfare of the United States.

Significantly, in addition to the Congressional powers enumerated above, the Constitution reinforces the role of Congress by giving it the authority and mandate:

"To make all laws which shall be necessary and proper for carrying into execution the foregoing powers, and all other powers vested by this Constitution in the Government of the United States, or in any department or officer thereof."

That list of powers, as viewed by the Senate itself, is impressive. The President may initiate and demand an action, but Congress supplies the money. The Presidency has absolutely no taxing power. The President may decide to send troops into another nation, but can he if Congress has not legislated the recruitment, payment, and provision of those troops? Congress holds the purse strings. The Constitution says it unequivocally.

Then, one must ask incredulously, how come the Symington subcommittee could react with such dismay at Presidential commitment of the United States in Thailand, Laos, Ethiopia, Spain, and thirty-nine other nations. The President commands an army of three-and-a-half million men scattered in thousands of bases around the world. If Congress appropriates the funds for those troops, how could Congress be so surprised and concerned about the uses made of them?

Author Tristram Coffin, writing in the *Bulletin of the Atomic Scientists* in 1967, gave a rather brutal answer:

. . . Congress has been glad to shove on the President the duties and headaches of foreign policy. Few members have been willing to do their homework on foreign policy, saying this wasn't the way to keep the voters happy.

Words granting or claiming Presidential powers over foreign relations have been uttered many times.

Thomas Jefferson: "The transaction of business with foreign nations is executive altogether." The Supreme Court has called the President's powers in the conduct of foreign policy "delicate, plenary and exclusive." Kenneth Waltz, writing in *Foreign Policy and Democratic Politics*, feared Congressmen

> may harry the officials and the diplomats who need time to think, may frighten them into timidity where boldness is required and block their attempts to move with subtlety to meet complex and shifting situations whose implications most Congressmen are not equipped to comprehend.

Dean Acheson, Secretary of State under Truman, told a congressional committee, "The argument as to who has the power to do this, that or the other thing is not exactly what is called for from Americans in this critical juncture." In 1961, Senator Fulbright, who certainly would wish to retract the statement now, warned Congress that "for the existing requirements of American foreign policy we have hobbled the President by too niggardly a grant of power."

Nicholas Katzenbach, Undersecretary of State for Johnson, told Congress, "His [the President's] is the responsibility for controlling and directing all the external aspects of the nation's power." He said the declaration of war, which under the Constitution can be voted only by Congress, "has become outmoded."

President Johnson, in commenting upon the 1964 Tonkin Gulf resolution passed by Congress which authorized him to take all steps he thought necessary in Vietnam, said, "We stated then, and we repeat now, we did not think the resolution was necessary to do what we did and what we're doing." President Nixon has made a similar statement.

Many other statements of Presidential power might be quoted, but one more will suffice. Everett M. Dirksen, late Republican leader in the Senate, said in 1967, "I have run down many legal cases before the Supreme Court [and] I have found as yet no delimitation on the powers of the Commander in Chief under the Constitution."

Not only did Presidents claim exclusive power in foreign affairs, but Congress granted it. No better statement of congressional acquiescence exists than that of Senator Fulbright on the last day of 1970:

> For many years the role exercised by the Committee on Foreign Relations was that of the unquestioning advocate of policies and programs submitted to the Senate by the Executive Branch of the Government. Regardless of the political complexion of the Executive or the Congress, the Committee—albeit with minor exceptions —tended to go along with the "facts" presented, the analysis of those facts, and the policy conclusions drawn therefrom by the Administration. . . . The emphasis in the Senate's role in "advise and consent" was on consent. In short, for many years the Committee *got along*

with the Executive Branch of the Government because it *went* along. [His emphasis.]

The Senate "went along" even when its most solemn power in foreign affairs, the ratification of treaties, was eroded to the point of virtual nonexistence. A succession of Presidents since Franklin Roosevelt have bypassed the Senate by making "executive agreements" with other nations. In 1940, Roosevelt sent twelve treaties to the Senate, but made twenty executive agreements. In 1944, he sent a single treaty for ratification, but negotiated seventy-four executive agreements.

The trend is reflected in the chart below:

YEAR	TREATIES	EXECUTIVE AGREEMENTS
1963	6	248
1964	13	231
1965	5	197
1966	10	242
1967	10	218
1968	57	226

With few exceptions the treaties submitted to the Senate were exceedingly minor. Fulbright addressed himself to the treaties President Nixon submitted to the Senate in 1970:

> . . . it is interesting to reflect that of the 27 treaties submitted . . . 10 had been negotiated by previous administrations (one indeed by the Coolidge administration); another 8 were routine bilateral extradition, double

taxation and consular conventions; 5 were concerned with trivia; one terminated a 1914 canal route treaty; and only 3 could be said to be breaking some new ground—those dealing with oil pollution on the high seas.

In fact, I voted "present" on one of the treaties, not because I was against it on the merits—it involved a minor payment to Canada for flood control benefits—but because I wanted to register my opposition to the shabby use of the treaty-making process.

At the same time that Congress was neglecting its Constitutional role in foreign affairs it was appropriating hundreds of billions of dollars for governmental machinery, much of it secret, which enormously enhanced the war powers of the President.

Most of the money went to create the world's foremost military machine, an Army, Navy, and Air Force of millions equipped with atomic weapons and the missiles and planes to carry them, ships, tanks, guns, and a bewildering and secret array of electronic gadgetry.

Military preparedness was one motive for these vast expenditures. Until 1950, United States policy was the exact opposite of military preparedness. The nation had only a minuscule Army, Navy, and Air Force. After each war, the military machine was dismantled as the nation returned to "normalcy."

Numerous events changed national attitudes. Americans believed the aggressions of Nazi Germany, Fascist Italy, and Japan in the 1930s could have been foiled by a display of military force. World War II could have been prevented if the dictatorships had been thwarted in their military adventures early. After North Korea invaded South Korea in 1950 and the United States was shown to be unprepared militarily to do much about it, the nation embarked on a policy of always being prepared to fight aggression.

Then there was the nation's morbid fear of Communism dating back to the Bolshevik Revolution in Russia in 1917. Many Americans believed that the Bolsheviks were determined to overthrow the American free enterprise system and enslave Americans in a dictatorship. In large measure, this fear was rooted in fact. Communism was imperialistic, seeking to control other nations by subversion or direct aggression. But in part the fear was irrational. At various times since 1920, hysteria has gripped the nation. Communist conspiracies have been "seen" when little evidence existed. A large number of politicians have sought notoriety by campaigning against the Communist "menace." The outstanding example was the late Senator Joseph McCarthy of Wisconsin, who claimed Communists were sequestered in every nook and cranny of the capital. No shred of evidence for his allegations was ever developed. Richard Nixon made his early political reputation as a Communist-baiting congressman. As a people, Americans came to see "Commie" conspiracies abroad as well as at home. If an oppressive, reactionary foreign government could blame its social and political opposition on Communist agitators, the United States might rush to its defense. The threat of "Communism" became an almost unfailing guarantee of American military and economic aid.

57

Our national fear of Communism and our determination to participate in international affairs led to the nation's becoming the world's policeman. We were ready, in the words of Kennedy's inaugural address in 1961, "to pay any price, bear any burden . . . to assure the survival and success of liberty." And readiness meant military preparedness.

Another reason for the vast expenditures for the military was economic and political advantages. Most of the money is spent in individual states and congressional districts. Members of Congress dearly love to cite at campaign time how much defense spending they brought to their area. Conversely, they dread accusations that they did not bring enough. In 1962, the Portland *Oregonian* chided the then Senator Wayne Morse of Oregon in these terms: "Washington State's *working* Senators won a billion dollars in military spending in one year for their people. . . . Oregon's talking senator has won only 6½ per cent of what Washington received."

Ken Hechler, a West Virginia congressman, rose in the House to state:

> I am firmly against the kind of log rolling which would subject our defense program to narrowly sectional or selfish pulling and hauling. But I am getting pretty hot under the collar about the way my state of West Virginia is shortchanged in Army, Navy and Air Force installations. . . . I am going to stand up on my hind legs and roar until West Virginia gets the fair treatment she deserves.

The late L. Mendel Rivers, former chairman of the

House Armed Services Committee, was once chided by an admiring colleague for securing defense installations for his district in South Carolina. Someone remarked that if the district got one more installation it would sink into the sea from the weight.

Senator Jacob Javits of New York, who as a member of the Foreign Affairs Committee is among the staunchest advocates of curbs on Presidential war powers, loudly complained in the past because New York got only 9.9 percent of military procurement while California claimed 23.9 percent.

For both high-minded motives and political ones a succession of Congresses, by bending hard to the task of military preparedness, have given enormous power to the President as Commander in Chief.

Congress has equipped the President with an immense intelligence apparatus of spies and information-gathering personnel and devices. This apparatus includes the Central Intelligence Agency, the intelligence arms of the Defense, State, and Justice departments, and the Atomic Energy Commission. Together they spend $3.5 billion a year to collect strategic intelligence about the Soviet Union, Communist China, and other countries that might harm the United States. Sometimes, the intelligence gathered is simply of interest to the United States; indeed, the nation has been known to spy on its closest allies.

By its very nature all this intelligence apparatus is secret. The very fact of the existence of much of it is not publicly acknowledged. The CIA headquarters in Virginia outside of Washington is unmarked and guarded.

A motorist who accidentally comes upon it is turned away. A similar situation exists at the headquarters of the National Security Agency in Maryland. It employs thousands of people in preparing codes and ciphers and breaking those of other nations. What these two agencies do, not to mention the Pentagon intelligence services, is rarely discussed in public, nor is it known beyond an extremely narrow group of people around the President. As one knowledgeable Washingtonian put it, "Everytime Richard Helms, the director of the CIA, coughs it is deleted from the record of Congressional testimony."

Why has Congress deliberately and knowingly given these secret powers to the President? Congress has provided the President with sources of information that no one in Congress, let alone the general public, has access to. Congress fostered the idea that the President knew more than anyone else and thus must be acting wisely, correctly, morally, and in the best interests of the nation. If someone had sat up nights thinking of ways to invest a leader with great powers, he would invent a secret intelligence system reporting to that leader. That is exactly what Congress did.

Presidential influence over criticism provides another reason for congressional compliance. In the late 1940s, President Truman instituted the principle of a "bipartisan foreign policy," which his successors happily embraced. Americans might quarrel over domestic policies, but we presented a united front expressed by a single voice, the President's, in our dealings with other nations. But there wasn't very much disagreement on foreign policy. Only rarely was criticism voiced. To do so was to violate the principle of a bipartisan foreign policy. The critic was risking charges of lack of patriotism, of sacrificing the nation and its goals for the benefit of personal, political gain. If someone sat up nights trying to think of a way to silence criticism and discussion, he would have invented the notion of a bipartisan foreign policy.

The President, declared by one and all to be the nation's sole spokesman and executor of foreign affairs, was granted what Theodore Roosevelt called a "bully pulpit" to express his views. On radio and television he could go directly to the people to make known the information he wanted made known and to explain the actions he proposed, or more often had already taken, to defend and protect the United States in his role as Commander in Chief and chief diplomat.

In any such presentation, two words were of cardinal importance. First, *defense:* The President would report that he was defending the United States and liberty against Communism. Given the climate of public and congressional opinion, defense could not be faulted.

The second key word was *crisis.* Depression, war, and the cold war with the Soviet Union created a series of crises in which Presidents felt compelled to act dramatically and forthrightly in the nation's interests. Historian Henry Steel Commager, writing in 1968, observed:

> We do not now take up arms because "American blood has been shed on American soil," nor does the President respond to an inescapable emergency such as the attack on Ft. Sumter. Now our President acts to "contain communism," to frustrate an "international conspiracy,"

to protect something vaguely called "vital interests" in far corners of the globe. . . .

It is not only concepts like "defensive" and "offensive" warfare or "vital interests" or "territorial waters" that are outmoded. Undersecretary Katzenbach has now formally asserted to the Senate Foreign Relations Committee that declarations of war are equally outmoded, thus neatly repealing a clause in the Constitution without the bother of congressional and state action. . . .

Four times in the past seven years Presidents have mounted major military interventions without congressional authority, on the plea of emergency: the Bay of Pigs, the [Cuban] missile crisis, Santo Domingo, and Vietnam. Only one of these—the missile crisis—could claim to be a genuine emergency, and, in a larger sense, even this was an emergency of our own making, for it is arguable that the whole Cuban muddle was a product of our miscalculations about Batista and Castro.

No example of Presidential use of mass communications stands out more than the raid on Son Tay in North Vietnam in December, 1970. By any rational system of measurement the raid to liberate American war prisoners was a failure. American troops reached the camp by helicopter and left with only minor casualties, but they found no prisoners to liberate. In the days following the raid President Nixon and Defense Secretary Melvin Laird termed the raid a great success. The men involved were labeled heroes and their leaders were brought to the White House to be decorated personally by the President.

The President, by saluting the men's heroism, effectively removed from Congress the ability to criticize the whole operation. No one asked whether the raid constituted an invasion of North Vietnam by American ground troops or to ask what might have happened if the raiders had been trapped at Son Tay. Would the United States have felt compelled to send a rescue mission?

One cogent criticism of the raid came from an unidentified "Washington official" quoted by *Newsweek* magazine. He supposedly said, "We are merchandising what essentially remains one big flop."

Since 1967, the neglect, acquiescence, and mindless appropriations which led to expanded Presidential war powers have been under fire. The Senate Foreign Relations Committee in its report on the National Commitments resolution decried "the new generation of foreign policy experts who [encourage] the belief that foreign policy is an occult science which ordinary citizens, including members of Congress, are simply too stupid to grasp." The report condemned the use of crisis diplomacy to place "tremendous pressures upon members of Congress to set aside apprehensions as to the exercise of power by the Executive, lest they cause some fatal delay or omission in the nation's foreign policy."

Senator Sam Ervin, a Southern conservative, declared the revolt against Presidential warmaking meant simply "that the people will not support forever a policy which is made for them but without them."

Dr. Ruhl Bartlett, a scholar of diplomatic history, told a Senate committee:

The Senate may need to do something rather drastic on some occasion to make sure that its authority is understood and needs to be respected. It may be that the Senate will have to say to the President on some occasion, "We will not stand for this any longer."

Senator Aiken, the ranking Republican in that chamber, said:

I don't think we can excuse Congress, because over the past 20 or 25 years we found it easier to tell the Executive Branch to take care of this matter or that when it was really our responsibility. . . . I blame the Executive Branch for some of its mistakes, but nevertheless Congress has to share the guilt with them because we have been too negligent and too tolerant.

Senator Church of Idaho declared:

What would have been on my mind if President Johnson had said to a joint session of Congress that the government of North Vietnam had by stealth invaded and attacked the government of South Vietnam on a day that would live in infamy? I would have said, "Where is the evidence?"

Senator Fulbright said:

The Senate Foreign Relations Committee has become aware that it is no service to the nation to accept without question judgments made by the Executive. Indeed, many of our current difficulties might have been avoided if we had taken time to stop, look and listen.

Senator Symington spoke out similarly in protest:

Frequent assertions by government officials and commentators that the President determines foreign policy do not make it so, nor do these assertions amend the Constitution; and if this Government is to function with success under that document, the Congress must constantly keep in mind its own constitutional authority.

And Senator Church again:

The myth that the Chief Executive is the fount of all wisdom in foreign affairs today lies shattered on the shoals of Vietnam.

Neglect, politics of the log-rolling variety, and crisis psychology help to explain the growth of Presidential war powers, but they still do not report the process by which Presidents have gone to war. Whom did they consult in making their momentous decisions? What did they fear and what were their motivations? Is it even possible for the process to be known? These questions are asked in pursuit still of an answer to our first question, How did it happen?

Chapter 4
How Presidents
Went to War

In the summer of 1940, Europe was aflame and reeling under the onslaughts of the armored Panzer divisions of Hitler's Nazi Germany. On May 10, Hitler attacked France. In six weeks, he crushed what was thought to be the foremost military power in the world. So great was the Nazi victory that only by the "miracle at Dunkirk" were the British able to rescue their expeditionary forces from the continent. Britain, stunned, its army virtually without equipment, was left to fight on alone against the military colossus that had overrun most of Europe.

President Roosevelt sought to rally the American people to come to the aid or active defense of Britain. In a speech that June he said, "Some, indeed, still hold to the now somewhat obvious delusion that we of the United States can safely permit the United States to become a lone island . . . in a world dominated by the philosophy of force." Moreover, Roosevelt stressed that the "whole of our sympathies lie with those nations that are giving their lifeblood to combat" Nazi Germany and vowed, "We will extend to the opponents of force the material resources of this nation. . . ."

The words were easier said than the deed performed. There was in the United States a large, vocal, powerful isolationist group which argued that America should stay out of the European war and not waste its men and resources in the blood feuds that lay an ocean away. Such isolationist sentiment was strong in Congress.

While attempting to rally public support for his policies, Roosevelt early in June ordered Army Chief of Staff George C. Marshall to locate excess arms and equipment and have them shipped to England. Several hundred freight cars were loaded with vintage armaments, ammunition, and two hundred planes. Roosevelt had no direct authorization for such action, but under an old 1917 statute, the armament was sold to a private firm, which presumably transferred it to England.

But the armament was not enough. Britain needed ships to combat the German submarine menace. Half the British fleet had been damaged or lost. England wanted fifty overage American destroyers. In exchange, it agreed to allow the United States to establish naval bases on its possessions in the Caribbean.

On August 2, 1940, Roosevelt met with his cabinet to

consider how best to arrange the exchange of destroyers for bases. Roosevelt wrote in notes he made at the meeting:

> It was agreed that legislation to accomplish this is necessary, [but] if asked for by me without any preliminaries, [it] would meet with defeat or interminable delay in reaching a vote.

Roosevelt felt the matter would have to be handled adroitly, particularly since the nation was on the eve of a Presidential election campaign. He enlisted the aid of editor William Allen White, one of the nation's leading internationalists. White, a friend of Wendell Willkie, the Republican Presidential candidate, was to try to enlist Willkie's support. If Willkie could be won over, White would then attempt to persuade Joseph Martin, House Republican leader, and Senator Charles L. McNary, Willkie's running mate. With such high-level GOP support, Roosevelt would submit the destroyer-bases proposal to Congress. The President believed it vital to act.

The plan came a cropper. Willkie refused to make a definite commitment. Roosevelt then sought to test public opinion. He arranged for Ambassador William C. Bullitt to address the American Philosophical Society in Philadelphia on August 18. Bullitt warned that if Britain fell to Germany, America would be next: ". . . the destruction of the British Navy would be the turning of our Atlantic Maginot Line."

Reaction was mixed. Bullitt received twenty-two thousand letters applauding his speech, but isolationists turned on him in fury, calling him a "multimillionaire, New Deal warmonger" and denouncing his speech as "little short of treason." The Chicago *Tribune* warned that the sale of ships to England would be an act of war. "If we want to get into war, the destroyers offer us as good a way as any of accomplishing the purpose."

On August 11, *The New York Times* carried a letter to the editor signed by four prominent attorneys, one of whom was Dean Acheson, later to be Secretary of State. The lawyers argued that the destroyer deal could be consummated under existing law by Presidential action alone. Roosevelt asked his Attorney General for a legal opinion and got what he wanted. The Constitution bestowed on the President, as Commander in Chief, authority to proceed with an executive agreement, where the national defense was concerned, without the Senate approval required for treaties. On September 2, Roosevelt consummated the deal, calling it an "epochal and far-reaching act of preparation for continental defense in face of grave danger."

Roosevelt took many other actions in defense of Britain and in preparation for the war he felt certain was coming. He extended the United States territorial waters three hundred miles into the Atlantic, thus permitting American warships to convoy merchant vessels to Iceland. In July, 1941, he sent American troops to Iceland and Greenland. He initiated a vast lend-lease progam of aid to Britain and the Soviet Union. Some of these actions—lend-lease, for example—were approved by Congress after long debate, but most were executive actions of the President. The method used to conclude the destroyer deal set the pattern for later developments in President Roosevelt's administration. It also set a pattern for the Presidents that followed him into office.

On June 25, 1950, the North Korean Army invaded South Korea. Both nations had been established as part of the agreements ending World War II. The North came under Communist domination, the South under United States influence.

When news of the North Korean invasion reached the United States, President Truman was in his home in Independence, Missouri, enjoying a brief vacation. Secretary of State Dean Acheson telephoned the news. The President instructed him to request an immediate meeting of the United Nations Security Council to charge North Korea with aggression. Meanwhile, Truman quickly flew back to Washington.

Truman believed that the invasion was an act of outright aggression, an effort to absorb another nation by military force. He remembered the policy of appeasement prior to World War II, when Britain, France, and the United States stood by while Germany forcibly annexed Austria and Czechoslovakia, Italy invaded Ethiopia, and Japan swept into China, Southeast Asia, and other areas. The United States had come out of World War II with the belief that the war could have been prevented had aggression been met head-on in the beginning.

President Truman was met at Washington's National Airport by Secretary of State Acheson, Defense Secretary Lewis Johnson, and Army Secretary Frank Pace. They drove directly to the Blair House, which was being used as the Presidential residence while the White House was under repair. A meeting with principal advisers was begun immediately. Cabell Phillips, chronicler of the Truman Presidency, termed the meeting "as momentous a conference on national strategy as he [Truman] had ever participated in."

The group had dinner and then went to work. They discussed all the intelligence information on the events in Korea, as well as South Korea's ability to defend herself. Acheson read various recommendations that had been offered. Truman chose three for immediate action: General Douglas MacArthur, the Supreme Commander in the Far East, was to send all planes and ships required to evacuate American civilian personnel from Korea and to use fighter planes to protect those operations; he was to get as much ammunition and other supplies as possible into the hands of the South Korean Army; and the United States Seventh Fleet was to move from the Philippines into the Formosa Strait to prevent spread of the conflict to that area.

Those were only the first steps. In ensuing days, after the United Nations Security Council voted 9–0 (Russia was absent by her own choice) to combat the aggression by all means possible, Truman ordered American planes, ships, and ground troops into action. The United States began a war that dragged on for three years.

Truman's actions in Korea were taken while Congress was not in session. There was great need for speed if North Korea was to be prevented from overrunning the whole peninsula and to call Congress into session would have taken time. The United Nations gave the President a legal authority. Relations with the UN are almost entirely an executive function. In appealing to that body and supporting its decision, the President was acting under international law.

Truman's decision not to ask for a congressional declaration of war against North Korea was of greater significance. That decision added debatable dimensions to Presidential war powers. He felt a formal declaration would lead, under the postwar skein of alliances, to similar declarations by the Soviet Union and China, thus causing World War III. Robert A. Taft of Ohio, the Republican leader of the Senate, raised the constitutional question of Congress' right to declare war. To the question, "Are we or are we not at war?", Truman replied, "We are not at war." In his view, the United States was simply helping South Korea "suppress a bandit raid." A reporter asked if it would be correct to call it "a police action." Truman replied, "Yes, that is exactly what it amounts to."

In 1958, the Middle East was in turmoil. Gamal Abdel Nasser had come into power in Egypt on a wave of nationalism. He was accepting aid from the Soviet Union and he threatened European interests in the Suez Canal. In 1956, Britain, France, and Israel had joined to invade Egypt and seize the Canal. President Eisenhower, standing on high moral ground, had rebuked those nations, our principal allies. "We do not accept the use of force as a wise and proper instrument for the settlement of international disputes . . ." he said. "There can be no peace without law." Nor could the United States insist on one standard for the nation's friends, another for its rivals.

In the uncertain political situation in the Middle East, Eisenhower had told Congress on January 5, 1957, that the United States could not afford "to leave a vacuum in the Middle East and prayerfully hope that Russia will stay out." He asked for 200 million dollars in economic and military assistance for the region and for authority to use armed force "to secure and protect the territorial integrity and political independence of such nations requesting such aid against overt armed aggression from any nation controlled by International Communism."

It is interesting that at the time Eisenhower was criticized by members of Congress who stated that in seeking the congressional approval the President was shirking his responsibility that constitutionally belonged only to him. Eisenhower defended his action saying he wanted the congressional resolution as evidence of America's nonpartisan solidarity. After two months of wrangling, the resolution was passed, but it contained no reference to congressional authorization.

The Eisenhower proposal came to be applied in Lebanon, which had a pro-Western government under President Camille Chamoun. It was a shaky government at best. Lebanon was rent with religious and tribal animosities. Various factions from inside the nation as well as from other Arab nations in the area were determined to topple Chamoun.

On May 13, Eisenhower met with Secretary of State

John Foster Dulles and others to discuss a communication from Chamoun inquiring "what our actions would be if he were to request our assistance." There was a great deal of discussion. It was felt that if the United States sent troops into the Middle East, an oil pipeline across Syria might be blown up, the Suez Canal might be blocked, and other Arab nations would find it impossible, in view of Arab resentment against the United States, to cooperate with us even if they wanted to. Eisenhower did not believe Russia would take any action if "the United States movement was decisive and strong." Eisenhower concluded from the discussion that John Foster Dulles favored direct action while his brother, Allen, the head of the CIA, favored caution and delay.

In the end Chamoun was told that the United States would respond directly and strongly to a request for troops *only* under certain conditions. First, Americans would not come in to achieve a second term for Chamoun. Second, another Arab nation would have to concur in the request for U. S. intervention. And finally, the purposes of our intervention would be to protect the lives and property of Americans and to assist the legal Lebanese government. Meanwhile, the U. S. Sixth Fleet was moved into the eastern Mediterranean and airborne troops in Europe were put on alert.

This crisis passed and Chamoun maintained control without United States intervention. Then on May 22, Chamoun took the matter to the United Nations Security Council. After debate, the UN decided to send a commission to Lebanon. By June 18, a forty-eight-hour truce had been arranged. Eisenhower supported the UN actions and seemed relieved to let that body handle the crisis. By early July it seemed the Lebanese crisis had passed.

Then, on July 14, a Communist coup toppled the pro-Western government of Iraq, creating a renewed crisis. As Eisenhower explained it, he had been counting on Iraq to maintain the stability of the area. That hope was now shattered. Eisenhower began to confer with the Dulles brothers and other military and diplomatic aides. Chamoun had requested United States military intervention within forty-eight hours and expressed annoyance that such aid had not been sent already. The conference continued with detailed discussion of the entire situation in the Middle East and predictions of the reactions in Europe, Russia, and the U. S.

In the afternoon of July 14, Eisenhower met with a bipartisan group of twenty-two congressional leaders in his office. All were briefed by the Dulles brothers. There was a discussion. Some members of Congress favored direct intervention, others urged caution. Speaker Sam Rayburn feared the United States was getting involved in a purely civil war in Lebanon. Senator Fulbright doubted seriously that the crisis was Communist-inspired. Eisenhower summed up his reaction to the meeting in these words from his book *Waging Peace*:

> At the end . . . I felt sure that Congress, while not attempting to impede our intervention in Lebanon, would not, in the absence of some greater emergency, support any more extensive action than had been discussed at

the meeting. *Except for a very few . . . none of the leaders was outspoken in his support of intervention in Lebanon; but authority for such an operation lay so clearly within the responsibility of the Executive that no direct objection was voiced. In any event, the issue was clear to me—we had to go in.* [Emphasis added.]

And he did, sending eventually 14,000 troops into Lebanon.

In the fall of 1962, the United States, by aerial surveillance and other means, detected the presence of Russian nuclear missiles in Cuba, ninety miles off our shores. The result was the famous Cuban missile crisis, an "eyeball-to-eyeball" confrontation between President John F. Kennedy and Soviet Premier Nikita Khrushchev.

On October 16, the President had irrefutable proof the Soviet missiles were in Cuba. There followed six days in which the world teetered on the brink of what Professor Sidney Warren has called an "unspeakable catastrophe." What stands out in the crisis is the time. The President had six whole days in which to act. The intelligence information he had was successfully kept from the public and Congress, giving him time to study, consider, argue, and seek the best solution to what he considered a most dire threat to the nation's security.

Kennedy and his advisers felt to a man that the Soviet missiles could not be allowed to exist so close to our shores, even though the Russians had been living in the opposite situation for years. The only question was how best to get rid of the missiles. Three basic alternatives were proposed: a military strike, a naval blockade, or a diplomatic bargaining session in which the United States would offer to remove some of its missiles confronting Russia in exchange for the Russian removal of theirs from Cuba.

On Friday, October 19, Kennedy met with the Joint Chiefs of Staff, who favored a military strike. Theodore Sorensen, in his book *Kennedy*, reports that the President left the meeting "impatient and discouraged." He was "counting on the attorney general [his brother, Robert Kennedy] and me, he said, to pull the group together quickly—otherwise more delays and dissension would plague whatever decision he took."

That same Friday night, Robert Kennedy and Sorensen met with a group of advisers to argue over the relative merits of a military strike versus a blockade. They could not agree, although the blockade seemed to be favored. Sorensen set out to write a speech for Kennedy that seemed an amalgamation of both alternatives.

During these deliberations President Kennedy had been campaigning in the Midwest. On Saturday afternoon he returned to the White House and met in his office with about fifteen trusted advisers. It was an informal group which later was labeled the executive committee of the National Security Council. Various people present argued the alternatives. In the end, the President chose the blockade because it could force the Russians to back down and still "save face."

But the diplomatic solution to the problem also had its advocates. In essence, the United States could offer to give up the American naval base at Guantanamo, Cuba, or certain missile sites in Turkey and Italy—none of which was very valuable to us—in exchange for the removal of the offending Russian missiles in Cuba. The advocates of negotiation said such an offer would not sound "soft," but, properly worded, would sound "wise." Kennedy rejected negotiation, saying concessions at that time would disturb America's allies by proving to them we would sacrifice their security to protect our own interests. He preferred to see the United States indict the Soviet Union for threatening world peace.

On Saturday afternoon and Sunday morning our allies in Latin America and Europe were informed of our plans, and desperate efforts were made to keep American journalists from breaking the news of the crisis.

On Sunday at 2:30 P.M., the National Security Council met again to go over all the plans for the blockade and to go over page by page the speech the President was to deliver to the nation Monday evening. Word by word, nuance by nuance, the speech was discussed so as to achieve exactly the proper effect desired by the President and his advisers. The President continued to work on the speech Sunday evening.

On Monday, Kennedy conferred with former Presidents Hoover, Truman, and Eisenhower, his own advisers, and his cabinet. In the afternoon, Secretary of State Rusk informed the Soviet Ambassador of the President's speech and showed him photographic evidence of Soviet missiles. Latin American governments were warned of possible riots and American ambassadors to those nations were advised to tape their windows in anticipation of violence.

At 5 P.M. Kennedy, the Secretaries of State and Defense, and the CIA Director briefed twenty-some congressional leaders, who had been flown to Washington from various parts of the country where they were campaigning or vacationing. Many did not favor blockade. Sorensen said Senators Richard Russell and Fulbright urged an invasion of Cuba. Representative Charles Halleck wanted the record to show that he had been informed at the last minute, not consulted. Despite differing opinions, Sorensen stated:

> *The President, however, was adamant. He was acting by Executive Order, Presidential proclamation and inherent powers, not under any resolution or act of Congress. He had earlier rejected all suggestions of reconvening Congress or requesting a formal declaration of war, and he had summoned the leaders only when hard evidence and a fixed policy were ready.* [Emphasis added.]

Sorensen said the President left the hour-long meeting angry, saying, "If they want this job, they can have it—it's no great joy to me."

The rest is history. The President made his speech at 7 P.M. and instituted the blockade. The Russians backed down and removed their missiles.

In 1965, the United States once again became involved in troop movements in the Caribbean, this time in the Dominican Republic. It was an immensely complicated situation, but the major U. S. involvement began with the assassination of Rafael Trujillo on May 30, 1961. For three decades he had been a repressive dictator. With his murder, the island nation erupted into revolution. A succession of individuals assumed or claimed control of the government. In 1961, President Kennedy sent eight ships loaded with eighteen hundred Marines to anchor off the shores of the republic, as a gesture of support for Joaquin Balaquer, a strong man who Kennedy believed could best rule the nation.

Political turmoil in the island seemed rooted in three warring factions: conservative militarists who believed only a strong, repressive government could control the nation; liberal democratic elements who wanted to establish an elected, progressive government; and Communists and Communist sympathizers.

In 1962, Juan Bosch was elected President. His program of social reform has been described as "uneven." Kennedy and his advisers considered him rather weak and susceptible to Communist influence. When Bosch was overthrown in September, 1963, Reid Cabral seized power in collaboration with the military. The situation erupted on Saturday, April 24, 1965, with open fighting between forces loyal to the exiled Bosch and the new Cabral government. In truth, the situation was vastly complicated with plots and subplots and with military officers fighting first on one side and then on the other.

In the muddled situation, the American Embassy in Santo Domingo reported that the Bosch forces were controlled by Communists and that they were winning. President Johnson felt that he must not permit a second Communist government to be established in the Caribbean. He was also concerned about the lives of Americans trapped by the fighting on the island. Johnson convened a meeting of the National Security Council and reportedly said:

> It's just like the Alamo. Hell, it's like if you were down at the gate and you were surrounded and you damn well needed somebody. Well, by God, I'm going to go—and I thank the Lord that I've got men who want to go with me, from [Defense Secretary Robert] McNamara right on down to the littlest private who's carrying a gun.

He ordered Marines on to the island. They began to arrive on April 28. Their number eventually rose to twenty-one thousand.

Two major questions remain unanswered to this day about this exercise in Presidential war powers. First, to what extent were Communists involved in the revolution in the Dominican Republic? Richard J. Walton wrote in *Beyond Diplomacy*:

> The American press began to descend on Santo Domingo and the Embassy immediately tried to convince them of the Communist character of the rebellion. The correspondents were given a list of 53 Communists and fellow travelers allegedly active in the revolution. This list became famous, to the acute embarrassment of the Johnson Administration, for it soon turned out that the list weakened rather than strengthened the United States argument. The Embassy didn't know that any of them had actually appeared in high-level positions in the rebel command but suggested that probably they had succeeded in concealing their influence. Then it turned out that some of the people on the list were not

Communists at all, and that several of them weren't even in the country when the revolution broke out.

In *The Tragedy of Lyndon Johnson,* Eric F. Goldman sought to portray the President's thinking on this issue:

Observers disagreed concerning how many and how influential they [the Communists] were; to LBJ, that was not the point. There were *some;* they *might* take over the revolution. No more Cubas . . . [Emphasis his.]

The second issue was the nature of the fighting and the danger to Americans. W. Tapley Bennett, the American Ambassador, told reporters of rebel atrocities of the head-severing variety. Reporters could not find much evidence to support the claim. But they did find Marines fighting in support of the Cabral forces when Johnson was declaring American noninterference in the political affairs of the country.

The famous telegram from Bennett to the President said, in part, "American lives are in danger. . . . If Washington wishes they [American troops] can be landed for the purpose of protecting evacuation of American citizens. I recommend immediate landings."

In a speech on May 3, President Johnson quoted this telegram as reading, "You must land troops immediately or . . . American blood will run in the streets." On June 17, Johnson explained to the nation:

Some 1,500 innocent people were murdered and shot, and their heads cut off, and six Latin American embassies were violated and fired upon over a period of four days before we went in. As we talked to our ambassador to confirm the horror and tragedy and the unbelievable fact that they were firing on Americans and the American embassy, he was talking to us from under a desk while bullets were going through his windows and he had a thousand American men, women and children assembled in the hotel who were pleading with their President for help to preserve their lives.

Most American newsmen reported that no embassy had been fired upon, no one had been beheaded, no considerable loss of life was visible, and no American civilian was hurt.

These conflicting viewpoints are reported here to illustrate the difficulties a President has in obtaining information on chaotic affairs in a distant part of the world—information on which he must base his personal decision on whether to use American military forces in a combat situation as well as the difficulties the American people and Congress have in evaluating how a President uses his war powers.

The war in Vietnam, or as it has become, the war in Southeast Asia is a long and complicated subject. It is a classic case of "creeping commitment." In 1954, Eisenhower dispatched economic and military aid to the government of South Vietnam, a corrupt and inefficient administration confronted by a rebellion. There was undoubted Communist influence from Russia and China among the insurgents, but the extent of it in those early days may never be known accurately. In the view of many people, the conflict in South Vietnam bore the characteristics more of a civil war than a Communist conspiracy. Many others, including four successive Presidents of the United States, disagreed.

When Eisenhower left office there were eight hundred military advisers in South Vietnam. When Kennedy was assassinated there were seventeen thousand. Even more amazing is the fact this commitment crept upward without any great personal involvement of American Presidents. Kennedy admitted that he had not paid much attention to Vietnam. It simply seemed less important than many other matters.

Involvement in a land war in Asia probably ranked at the bottom of a hypothetical list of things that President Johnson personally wanted. He had won the greatest Presidential victory in history in 1964 by criticizing Republican Barry Goldwater for proposing active American military action in the war [though The Pentagon Papers reveal that Johnson himself expected the war to accelerate]. But, how did Johnson achieve what he did not want?

One key explanation is the belief, held by every President since Truman, that aggression must be repelled. Johnson felt, as had Eisenhower and Kennedy, that although the strife in South Vietnam bore many characteristics of a civil war, there was a great deal of evidence that Russia, China, and North Vietnam were encouraging the insurgents and actively aiding them with the aim of a Communist take-over in South Vietnam. That constituted aggression.

Johnson also inherited policies from previous Presidents.

When he took office it had been established as policy that anti-Communist governments must be bolstered all over the world regardless of their nature and that the United States had a duty to make sacrifices to contain the march of communism by whatever means necessary. To this mix was added an attitude which every President feels—Johnson more than his predecessors. Among his highest duties, Johnson ranked the protection of Americans and the "flag" wherever they were on this earth.

All of these attitudes combined to deepen American involvement despite the President's expressed wishes to the contrary. Successive governments of South Vietnam proved hopelessly inept in coping with the Viet Cong insurgents. The United States was pouring money, materials, and men into the fray and steadily losing. National pride and the compulsion to thwart "aggression" led to greater and greater aid and ultimately to active combat participation. When television cameras showed shocking pictures of wrecked American planes and dead and dying American soldiers, pure patriotism drove the American people and their President to defend the flag and punish aggressors.

In 1964, following the "attack" on American destroyers in the Gulf of Tonkin, Congress formally resolved that it approved and supported "the determination of the President, as commander in chief, to take all necessary measures to repel any armed attack against the forces of the United States and to prevent further aggression."

Another key was the notion held that the vast military power of the United States, if merely threatened, let alone actually used, could compel an "aggressor" to surrender or at least negotiate. North Vietnam was among the world's weakest nations. It simply did not make sense to the American mind that North Vietnam would persist in the face of American "determination." But it did. It continued to do so under intensive American air raids. It neither surrendered, stopped its activities, nor showed any willingness to negotiate other than on its own terms. The misjudgment of the will of the North Vietnamese will rank as one of the great miscalculations in American history. Previously the United States had accomplished its goals by sending a naval squadron or landing a few Marines.

Finally the tragic war in Southeast Asia led to the great debate over Presidential war powers. Senator Fulbright, a long time friend and supporter of President Johnson, broke with him on the war issue, withdrew his earlier support, and openly criticized the President. His comments, swelled by the voices and views of hundreds of thousands of others, made war power a national issue.

This discussion of the war in Vietnam was written prior to the publication of excerpts from The Pentagon Papers. In gray column after gray column of reports from those papers, there is nothing which calls for the alteration of this necessarily brief account of how we got into the war.

The papers themselves are something else. They were collected and written in 1968 by the order of Defense Secretary McNamara. There is speculation that he did this because of his personal disillusionment with the war and because of his desire to leave a record for future historians. But McNamara has not said why he did it. Until he does, speculation is senseless. He did it. The papers were classified "top secret-sensitive." Fifteen copies were printed. Since the papers extended to 47 volumes containing 4 million words, it is hardly remarkable that practically nobody read the entire study. (In this book you are reading only 50,000 words.)

What happened next either is not known or has not been made known. One or more people decided to steal, photocopy the documents and release them to the press. Daniel Ellsberg, a former Pentagon official who supposedly worked on preparation of the papers, has admitted doing this, according to press reports. The papers were turned over to selected newspapers in a cloak-and-dagger, straight-out-of-the-movie-spy-thriller fashion. Newspaper editors agonized over the "top secret" stamp on the documents, but decided to print what they figured to be the journalistic "scoop" of the century.

The federal government immediately tried to stop publication of the documents and stories based upon them. Government attorneys were temporarily successful in delaying publication, but ultimately the United States Supreme Court ruled that the government's action violated the Constitutional guarantee of freedom of the press.

The Pentagon Papers, as reported in the press, are immensely valuable. In view of the "top secret" designation on them—a designation which the Government was unable to convince successive judges was necessary—the papers probably would not have been published for decades. Because the papers are available now, the participants in the war-making decisions can comment and explain them. But it is monstrously unfortunate that the papers had to be stolen and published in the press in the manner that they were.

It is not too soon to start putting these papers into context. They are by no stretch of the imagination a "history." They are, at best, *evidence* for history. They were written over a period of time apparently by 40 different people who were given access to some (or possibly all) of the documents in the Department of Defense. At this writing, no one has identified the authors or what part of the papers they penned. Without that there can be no judgment of their qualifications to write and the effectiveness of what they have written. Initially it was assumed that they were writing a deliberately negative report on how the nation got involved in Vietnam. It does not seem to have occurred to anyone that instead of trying to make the government look "bad," they glossed over facts to make it look "good." Without a historian, there is no history.

The "history" is also grossly incomplete. The faceless, nameless authors did not have access to the files of the State Department and the White House, nor do we know whether they sought it. Many, perhaps most, of the major decisions were made in those two places. No interviews were made with the major participants in the decision-making processes, but were they sought? What is left are the memos, the letters, the notes, the orders, executed by people at the Department of Defense.

As a "history," the Pentagon Papers are so abysmally awful that one can but describe them as lousy. What documents, such as raw notes or conversations, influenced the decision-making powers?

But, lousy or not, incomplete, biased and whatever else they might be, The Pentagon Papers are shattering. Even if all the wrong documents were selected for all the wrong reasons, the sheer volume of them shows that many people in the Pentagon were sitting up nights promoting a war and deceiving the Congress, the American people and possibly even the President. The sum total is an unbelievable morass of stupidity, arrogance, miscalculation and plain deception.

The papers indicate—although they do not yet prove—that the United States propelled itself into the war on the basis of inconclusive evidence of Communist aggression; involved itself in provocative military forays against the North Vietnamese, while claming to be innocent; countered all efforts of the South Vietnamese to settle their civil war by negotiation; helped to topple South Vietnamese governments; engaged in military maneuvers, such as bombing the North, which were of dubious value to start with and continued them long after they were known to be of no use; concealed information from the Congress and the people; sought to manipulate Congress and public opinion for Executive purposes; lied, lied and still lied again, then mistated, concealed and deceived. The list of revelations from the papers could fill this whole book.

Tragically the presentation of The Pentagon Papers tends to destroy their value. The issue became lost in the question of freedom of the press. The newspapers grandly and sanctimoniously wrapped themselves in the

Constitution and forgot the original story. A second issue, the classification of government documents, was also obscured. Congressmen and columnists raced off to investigate and denounce the Government's process of classification.

The Pentagon Papers show at least part of the process and psychology by which the Executive Branch has taken the nation to war. They reveal the arrogance, the misinformation, the miscalculation which have led the nation to the longest, least liked war in its history. They offer massive fuel for the debate on Presidential powers. They are a mine of information on how those powers might be restricted for the good of the nation. They offer a chance for a return to greater democracy, with the people and Congress participating in the nation's affairs to a fuller extent. They offer us all a chance to learn—not only the value of a free press, or the need to declassify documents, but how we have become such a warlike nation.

Let us consider one more example of the Presidential use of war powers, President Nixon's decision to send American troops into Cambodia in May, 1970. Although it is virtually impossible to write about it with any accuracy now, much of the outcry over the Cambodia action stemmed from criticism of the manner in which the President was believed to have reached his decision.

Journalists reported that the President met with a small group of advisers, including Secretary of State William Rogers, Defense Secretary Laird, and National Security adviser Henry Kissinger. Doubtless he discussed the matter with the Joint Chiefs of Staff and intelligence experts. According to press reports, lower-echelon experts on Southeast Asia in the State and Defense departments were apparently not even informed, let alone consulted, about the decision.

The decision apparently was made with relative suddenness. Less than a week before the invasion Secretary Rogers had told a House appropriations subcommittee that:

> we recognize that if we became involved in Cambodia with our ground forces, our whole program is defeated. I think the one lesson that the war in Vietnam has taught us is that if you are going to fight a war of this kind satisfactorily, you need public support and congressional support.

After the invasion, a member of Congress said publicly, "If I were Rogers, I would resign."

The press also reported much speculation that both Rogers and Laird, if not opposed to the invasion, were lukewarm about it. The two men went to great lengths to deny this, however. Because the President neither consulted nor informed congressional leaders about the invasion, they reacted with outrage.

Nixon at least gave the contemporary impression that he committed American ground forces into Cambodia on the basis of a unilateral decision privately arrived at. This impression added great fuel to the debate over Presidential war powers.

But what of the mechanics of decision making, the administration of war powers? One final time—how did it happen?

Chapter 5
The Administration
of War Powers

THE PRESIDENT is not alone and therein lies both his power and limitations upon his power. He is surrounded by a vast establishment intimately involved in his war powers, both helping him to arrive at his decisions and in carrying them out.

In January, 1971, *The New York Times* published a list of United States government agencies which maintain personnel in foreign countries:

> American Battle Monuments Commission
> Agency for International Development
> Agriculture Department
> Atomic Energy Commission
> Bureau of Narcotics and Dangerous Drugs
> Central Intelligence Agency

Commerce Department
Customs Department
Defense Department
Environmental Science Services Administration
Export-Import Bank
Federal Aviation Administration
Federal Bureau of Investigation
Foreign Agriculture Service
General Services Administration
Health, Education and Welfare Department
Housing and Urban Development Department
Immigration and Naturalization Service
Interior Department
Internal Revenue Service
Justice Department
Labor Department
Maritime Administration
National Aeronautics and Space Administration
National Science Foundation
Peace Corps
Public Health Service
Smithsonian Institution
State Department
Tennessee Valley Authority
Transportation Department
Treasury Department
United States Information Agency
United States Travel Service
Veterans Administration.

The *Times* reported that each of these agencies has personnel attached to American embassies abroad "reporting through separate channels to different department heads who compete with the Washington bureaucracy for the car of the White House." The result, according to the State Department report, is a set of "incredibly numerous, frequently parochial, often overlapping and occasionally conflicting" interests.

Many of these agencies are involved in simple administration of American activities abroad, interests far removed from Presidential war powers. In this category are the American Battle Monuments Commission, the Narcotics Bureau, Customs Department, General Services Administration (which has charge of embassies and other buildings), and those agencies involved in the housing, health, transportation, and taxation of Americans abroad. But what is the connection between the Tennessee Valley Authority and foreign relations?

The key agencies that augment Presidential war powers are the Agency for International Development, Atomic Energy Commission, Central Intelligence Agency, Defense Department, State Department, and the United States Information Agency. All of these, as well as the rest to a greater or lesser extent, have a direct role in the administration of foreign affairs. To this list must be added one other key organization, the White House Executive Office. Here are sequestered many of the key advisers to the President, people who report directly and only to him.

This immense bureaucratic network possesses a size and array of activities both bewildering and unfathomable. School books tend to oversimplify: the State Department runs our foreign affairs, the Defense Department the military, etc., all under the direction of the President and, presumably, with his knowledge.

In truth, foreign relations are splashed all over the federal government and Presidential control is sporadic at best. Suppose that a relatively minor official in the Department of Agriculture decided not to buy a certain commodity that was essential to the economy of an African, Asian, or South American nation. Theoretically, in the wake of his decisions economic depression, revolt, a Communist take-over, missile deployment, and war might come. Lest it be thought this is farfetched, it might be well to remember that it has been charged that Castro Cuba was thrust into the arms of communism by the American decision to stop purchasing sugar from that nation.

Events on these far-flung diplomatic fronts have intimate relevancy to American foreign policy and commitments abroad, yet knowledge of these events seldom surfaces to public attention. Late in 1970, President Nixon was personally aghast and publicly embarrassed by the Coast Guard. While the U. S. was engaged in sensitive negotiations with the Russians over fishing rights in the Atlantic, officers permitted Soviet officers to board an American vessel to beat, bind, and carry off a Lithuanian sailor who had sought asylum on the vessel. Belatedly, the President disciplined the officers, but the incident indicates the absence of his control over events and policies at the edges of his diplomatic empire.

Tens of thousands of minor officials only distantly involved in considerations of war and peace are simply performing routine tasks that can become an issue for the entire nation. The President cannot do everything. He must delegate to others both the tasks and the authority to carry out those tasks. Tens of thousands of persons are now "delegates" in the performance of important tasks abroad.

An illustration is provided by the military-base agreement between Spain and the United States. Merlo J. Pusey, commenting upon the revelations in January, 1971, suggested the story be entitled, "How Not to Conduct Negotiations for Military Bases Abroad."

In 1968, the United States sought to extend the life of its bases in Spain, which had been built in the early 1950s. In return the Spanish government wanted a reported 1.2 billion dollars' worth of American weapons plus a joint security pact. The price seemed too high to State Department diplomats, and the talks bogged down. At this point, Secretary of State Rusk suggested to his Spanish counterpart that military leaders on both sides "develop common strategic concepts" that could later be followed by "political discussions."

General Earle Wheeler, chairman of the Joint Chiefs of Staff, and other officers went to Spain for talks. A subsequent memorandum seemed to indicate an agreement that joint Spanish–United States action would be employed against any threat to Spain from Africa. At this point, the State Department raised an eyebrow, for all this sounded very much like a joint security pact. But the problem then became to avoid causing the U. S. generals to lose face. A rewording of the negotiated preamble was worked out:

The present document on tasks and missions, as well as

the previous discussions at the military level, are not necessarily the views of the governments of Spain and the United States nor do they imply intergovernmental understandings or commitments between the two countries.

But in so far as President Nixon was concerned the damage had been done. The news of the possible alliance with Spain reached the press. The Senate Foreign Relations Committee was appalled. Hearings were held and the Senate passed its resolution denying any commitment between Spain and the United States, even though the administration repeatedly denied any had been intended.

So vast is the diplomatic bureaucracy that the President has difficulty learning what is going on, including how his orders are being carried out. The Symington subcommittee reported an "incredible duplication and waste" in Thailand, where "at one time the three military services, along with the Agency for International Development, the United States Information Agency and the CIA, were each operating independent counterinsurgency programs or were separately training Thais to operate them." The subcommittee said, "The Thais themselves apparently have never viewed the insurgency problem in the same magnitude as do the Americans."

At another point the subcommittee reported:

Costly and unnecessary duplication exists among the various United States intelligence agencies operating abroad. In at least one situation, two of our agencies were working with competing local agencies of a foreign country.

A succession of Presidents has struggled with the problem of simply administering foreign affairs. Kennedy openly declared his despair of making the State Department more responsive and innovative. He called it a "bowl full of jelly." Journalist Terence Smith reported in the *New York Times:*

> An instruction to an ambassador can require up to 27 signatures for clearance before it is dispatched. One new officer recently managed, by nagging everyone concerned, to put a moderately important cable through to an embassy in Southeast Asia in a week's time. He was astonished when more experienced colleagues applauded.
>
> Another officer, against his will, developed a fat folder of interdepartmental paper on the question whether the cotton yarn included in a certain country's aid program would be shipped on spindles or bales. "I was going out of my mind," he recalled, "so one day I just threw the folder away and made a decision. Spindles. I never heard another word about it."

The State Department is well aware of the hardening of its bureaucratic arteries. In a 610-page critique of itself, the department spoke of its "intellectual atrophy" and urged self-reforms to modernize its actions and thinking.

A succession of Presidents have grappled with ways to cope with the State Department. Two distinct methods have emerged. Journalist Don Oberdorfer of the Washington *Post* has suggested the different methods are one way to distinguish a Democratic from a Republican President. Kennedy and Johnson tended to administer in a free-wheeling manner, not hesitating to reach down to the lower ranks of the bureaucracy to telephone to a particular specialist who had information of value. Eisenhower and Nixon tend to operate more on a military-staff concept, creating administrative machinery in the White House to oversee the work of the various agencies.

Nixon has leaned heavily on Henry Kissinger, his special assistant for national security affairs. Kissinger, who heads a staff of 110 people (twice the number on President Roosevelt's whole White House war staff), stands literally at the President's side and is in close, daily contact. Nixon relies on Kissinger for information, advice, and coordination of the activities of the various diplomatic agencies.

There is a problem with either method. The President, because of human limitations of time and energy, can pay attention to only a few things at a time. In his first two years in office, Nixon gave the bulk of his attention to foreign affairs. But even with the indefatigable aid of Kissinger, his attention focused on the problems of Southeast Asia, the Middle East, Europe, and relations with Russia and China. The rest of the world, including Latin America, Africa, and the bulk of Asia was left to the ministrations of the State Department and other agencies.

One result is that the United States frequently speaks with conflicting voices. In 1970, the United States Information Agency broadcast descriptions of Soviet "duplicity" in the Middle East at a time when the State

Department was trying to negotiate with the Russians to achieve a greater compliance with the cease fire in the Suez Canal area. The State Department has gone on record as approving West German efforts to improve its relations with the Communist bloc. Kissinger, however, has expressed his doubts about the wisdom of the West German actions.

The President can only cope with immediate crises and hope that our relations with the rest of the world do not become too muddled. But muddled they sometimes become.

Even when a President is on top of a situation, as he frequently is, he may experience difficulties in having his policy carried out. His subordinates, out of disagreement with the policy or simple ineptitude, may "drag their feet," cause delays, make mistakes that undermine the policy, or simply ignore orders altogether. A President may order troops into a foreign country, but he cannot directly control the speed with which the troops are alerted, marched aboard transports, and shipped in accordance with his orders. If military officers are against the policy, they can engage in an astonishing variety of foot dragging. When Nixon determined to "Vietnamize" the war in Vietnam by preparing the South Vietnamese army to assume the burden of the fighting, he assigned the task to Defense Secretary Laird. Knowing that the military was lukewarm about the policy, Laird insisted that the ablest Pentagon officers be assigned to the program and demanded daily progress reports.

If the President has a problem in learning what is happening in international relations, Congress has an even greater problem. The Symington subcommittee complained bitterly that it simply could not get information. It verbally singed the executive branch for overclassifying, that is, making secret, essential information.

> The Executive Branch consistently over-classified information relating to foreign policy that should be a matter of public record. This is partly the result of bureaucratic timidity, especially at the middle and lower levels, where the prevailing approach is to look for some reason either to cover up or to withhold facts.

It said the secrecy sometimes occurs at the request of foreign governments which do not have a free press or responsible political opposition.

> The Government of Thailand did not want it known that the United States was using air bases in that country. The Government of Laos did not want it known that the United States was fighting in a major fashion in that country. Even in the Philippines where there is a free press and a highly articulate political opposition, the Government of the Philippines did not want it known that the United States was paying heavy allowances to the Philippine non-combat contingent that went to Vietnam.

But many times the classification is placed by American officials.

> Classification often permits an ambiguity about various commitments to be purposely developed by the Executive Branch. The practice often is to:
> Maximize commitment in secret discussions with for-

eign governments; then minimize the risk of commitment in statements made to the American public. Maximize in public the importance of our friendly relationship and cooperation with a foreign government; then minimize, and often classify, that government's obstructiveness, failures and non-cooperation. These actions make policy change and review both unlikely and politically difficult.

The Symington subcommittee then arrived at the heart of the issue:

Americans pride themselves on having an open society. Nevertheless, it is becoming an increasingly closed government. Yet neither the Congress nor the people can make intelligent judgments without questions which may literally involve our survival unless they have free access to all pertinent information which would not aid a possible enemy.

There is no merit to the argument that certain activities must be kept secret because a foreign government demanded they would be kept secret. Such a policy involves the Government of the United States in a web of intrigue which is alien to American traditions.

The subcommittee sought to illustrate this statement:

Everyone recognizes that national security imposes limits on the disclosure of information. Knowledge of much intelligence information deserves to be held, even within the government, by a relatively small number of people. But the multi-million dollar support of a 30,000 man [Laotian] army can in no way be considered an intelligence operation; and to try to keep it classified is to deny information to those who also have responsibility and authority for our defense structure and its functioning.

Another example: by classifying the number of daily missions flown by United States aircraft over northern Laos since 1964—as distinguished from those missions flown over the Ho Chi Minh Trail and thus directly connected to the Vietnam war—the Executive Branch hid from the Congress as well as the people that additional major commitment in men and dollars undertaken to support the Royal Government of Laos. . . .

The result of such effort to classify over here information that is available to the public overseas has contributed to a growing discontent among the American people as to the credibility of their own government.

The subcommittee accused the Administration of practicing "secrecy from Congress."

In at least one instance, security classification has been used to prevent legitimate inquiry by the proper committees of the Senate into matters which the Executive Branch did not want to discuss.

It spoke of "one striking instance" in which the Administration sought to restrict the Senate Foreign Relations Committee:

It was with great surprise . . . that the subcommittee found, when it began its hearings, that at the direction of the Executive Branch there was to be no discussion of nuclear weapons overseas.

Later, the committee was permitted a single-day, worldwide briefing on the weapons. But only one copy of the transcript was to be made and it was to be held by the State Department. It would be available to the Foreign Relations Committee only upon request.

President Nixon's efforts to inform himself and to control the nation's international affairs are intensifying Congress' information-gathering difficulties. By long tradition, the President and members of his immediate White House staff cannot be compelled to testify before Congress. Kissinger and his staff, as well as the new chairman of the Council on International Economic Policy, hold the rank of Presidential assistant and determine many of the nation's key foreign policies. Congress has no way to question them about their activities.

If the President has difficulty informing himself and Congress has even more difficulty, what of the people? The problem approaches the impossible at times. An illustration occurs in the transcript of hearings before the Senate Foreign Relations Committee in June, 1969. Page 7 of the transcript contains the following:

STATEMENT OF HON. RICHARD HELMS
DIRECTOR, CENTRAL INTELLIGENCE AGENCY
Mr. Helms. (Deleted).
The Chairman. Thank you, Mr. Director.

Preceding this the transcript contains an exchange of letters between Chairman Fulbright and Defense Secretary Laird, who wrote:

. . . it should be obvious that the deletion of Mr.

Helms' testimony from the public version creates certain grave obstacles to a balanced understanding of what transpired.

In his letter of reply to Laird, Fulbright wrote:

The deletion of all Mr. Helms' testimony, and of certain portions of your testimony, were made by the Executive Branch and not by the committee. If this procedure has resulted in what you consider to be an "incomplete" record which "creates grave obstacles to a balanced understanding of what transpired," to quote your letter, the responsibility for having brought about this result is surely yours and not mine.

The public's difficulties in finding out what is going on is further illustrated by this passage from the transcript of the Symington subcommittee's hearing on the American agreement with Spain. Elliot L. Richardson, then Undersecretary of State, now Secretary of Health, Education and Welfare, testified:

. . . at the risk of being a little tedious about it, I would call attention to the operative verb with the sentence beginning at the bottom of Page 1 of the February 27 minute. Skipping the irrelevant language, "The military representatives agree that any instance of aggression by"—skipping the people who may be responsible for the aggression, and then going over to the top of page 2, "directly affects and interests both countries, since they are common security interests." The next sentence is, "They further agree that any situation (deleted) may be of less direct concern to one or the other but may have indirect implications which would make it desirable to hold consultations between appropriate representatives of the countries." That is all the language says. It says that aggression by military forces of (deleted) or by (deleted) "proxy" military forces against the interest of both countries directly affects and interests both countries and, therefore, should be the subject of mutual consultations.

Someone may understand all that, but he is hardly likely to be a member of the general public who has been reading the transcript in search of enlightenment.

Chapter 6
Curbing
the War Powers

THE DEBATE OVER Presidential war powers poses two questions: Should Presidential powers be curbed? And, if so, how?

Powerful legal and practical arguments exist for not curbing the war powers. The Constitution declares the President to be Commander in Chief. That clause establishes civilian control by elected officials over the military. Today, with the nation possessing such a powerful military, few if any would doubt the wisdom of such an arrangement. We must ask, as Professor Clinton Rossiter has, "Where else . . . could it possibly have been placed?"

In generals and admirals? Hardly, in the American context of things. In a committee of distinguished civilian and military leaders? Various successful nations, including the Soviet Union, do this, but Americans have long had a distrust of government by committee. *Power held by a few, even if they are elected, is no more blessed or cursed than power held by a single person.* In Congress? The history of our nation, as many other nations, proves that in moments of national crisis a legislative body, no matter how efficient (which Congress is not), is poorly equipped to act forthrightly and courageously. To my knowledge, not even the most determined apostle of legislative authority has suggested that war powers be invested solely in Congress.

The President is Commander in Chief. He administers the laws. He is chief of state. He determines foreign policy and conducts it. Not even Senator Fulbright suggests that the Senate Foreign Relations Committee ought to conduct the nation's affairs with other countries. In an age of crises, real or imagined, few if any Americans would suggest any diminution of the ability of the President to act quickly and dynamically in the nation's interests.

Americans expect their elected President to be wise and courageous and to *lead.* Even when his purposes are unknown or misunderstood, even when he takes a difficult course which causes hardship for Americans, there is a sense of pride and a feeling of safety that a strong man is at the helm of the nation. The President was granted a four-year term and his removal from office was made difficult precisely so he would have the ability to make the hard choices that true leadership sometimes requires.

President Johnson, witnessing the decline in his popularity because of the war in Vietnam, declared he would continue his course even if his popularity dropped to 1 percent, because he believed that what he was doing was right. He decided, however, not to run for reelection.

Any American looking back over his nation's history must conclude that Americans have been served well by their Presidents. It might be said we could have been better served by a few of them, but none has become a dictator, none has failed to carry out his responsibilities, at least in some fashion, and none has destroyed the nation. Rather, the United States has become rich and powerful, and Presidents must be given at least some of the credit for that. Professor Rossiter has called the Presidency "one of the few truly successful institutions created by men in their endless quest for the blessings of free government." Professor Henry Steele Commager, addressing himself to the subject of Presidential war powers since Franklin Roosevelt, remarked:

> . . . we are forced to conclude that what we have is not a manifestation of personal or even official ambition, but something inherent in the Presidency and in the age in which these Presidents serve.

We may have been served well by Presidents, but have we been so served by a succession of Congresses? Since 1945, Congress has neglected its great Constitutional powers in foreign affairs and even beseeched Presidents to take the burden from them. Only recently has Congress sought to reaffirm its powers. The debate then, is not so much over the curbing of Presidents, but the invigoration of Congress. Senator Fulbright has pointed out that certain political scientists argue that the checks and balances formerly provided by Congress are now provided by various officials within the executive branch. He denounced this, quoting historian Ruhl J. Bartlett, who called it an argument "scarcely worthy of small boys." Bartlett went on:

> . . . the issue is not one of advice or influence. It is a question of power, the authority to say that something shall or shall not be done. If the President is restrained only by those whom he appoints and who hold their positions at his pleasure, there is no check at all. What has happened to all intents and purposes, although not in form or words, is the assumption by all recent Presidents that their constitutional right to conduct foreign relations and to advise the Congress with respect to foreign policy shall be interpreted as the right to *control* foreign relations. [Emphasis added.]

Senator Fulbright then said:

> I strongly believe that the Congress should undertake to revive and strengthen the deliberative function which it has permitted to atrophy in the course of 25 years of crisis. Acting on the premise that dissent is not disloyalty, that a true consensus is shaped by airing differences rather than by suppressing them, the Senate should again become, as it used to be, an institution in which the great issues of American politics are contested with thoroughness, energy and candor. Nor

should the Senate allow itself to be too easily swayed by executive pleas for urgency and unanimity, or by allegations of "aid and comfort" to the enemies of the United States made by officials whose concern with such matters may have something to do with a distaste for criticism directed at themselves.

It is sometimes useful and occasionally necessary for Congress to express prompt and emphatic support for the President on some matter of foreign relations. It seems to me, however, that we have gone too far in this respect, to the point of confusing Presidential convenience with the national interest. It is perfectly natural for the President, pressed as he is to make decisions and take action in foreign relations, to over-emphasize the desirability of promptness and unanimity. But the Senate has its own responsibilities, and however strongly feelings of patriotism may incline it to comply with the President's wishes, a higher patriotism requires it to fulfill its constitutional obligation.

Fulbright is among those members of Congress who would go beyond congressional debate over foreign policy. He was in the forefront of the debate that led to the resolutions forbidding the President from using American ground forces in Cambodia, Laos, and Thailand without congressional permission. His committee authored the National Commitments resolution, and the resolution denying an American commitment to Spain. Other measures debated in Congress have attempted to withhold funds to compel the President to withdraw American forces from Cambodia and even Vietnam.

All of these resolutions tend to tie the hands of the President in foreign affairs and national emergencies.

President Nixon believes that the process of extricating the United States from Vietnam will be better served by military excursions into Cambodia and Laos where North Vietnamese and Communist insurgents are operating. Critics have charged that Nixon is violating the spirit if not the letter of the congressional resolutions.

Clearly, those resolutions have made it more difficult for the President to carry out his military policies as Commander in Chief and have put the United States in the position of having South Vietnamese troops fight America's battles. Certainly, having South Vietnam invade a neighboring nation with American air support does not remove very much of the onus of aggression from the United States, if onus there is.

Second, such resolutions do not promise to be effective in restraining Presidents. The National Commitments resolution has been criticized on this ground by Professor Commager:

> Admirable as it is, this resolution holds out little hope of effectiveness. If it had been on the statute books at the time of the Tonkin Gulf episode or at the inception of our bombing of North Vietnam, would it have prevented or mitigated these actions? Surely not, for the Administration would have cited—as it does tirelessly—the "obligations" of the SEATO treaty, or it would have invoked the amorphous concept of "vital interest."
>
> Would the resolution have voided the Cuban missile crisis? No, because action at that time was not alleged to be based on a national "commitment," but on Presidential responsibility to defend the United States against attack.

Would it have stayed Eisenhower's intervention in Lebanon or the Pescadores? No, because these had Senate endorsement, after a fashion. Would it have avoided intervention in Guatemala in the early fifties, or the more notorious intervention in Santo Domingo in 1965? Probably not, for intervention in Santo Domingo—like that in Lebanon—was justified on the argument that American lives were in peril, while our Guatemalan adventure was so private that to this day the Congress seems unacquainted with it.

None of the resolutions thus offered can stay the President's hand. He can act in secret—as in Laos—and simply present the Congress and the nation with a *fait accompli*, justifying his action on his authority as Commander in Chief and his responsibility to protect the nation and its interest or to protect American lives. Or, he could simply break the law, explaining as Lincoln did in the Civil War, that it was better to break one law than have the nation destroyed. Or, he could offer as evidence of his sincerity, as Lyndon Johnson did, his refusal to seek another term in office.

Congress has no effective way to restrain Presidential power as Commander in Chief. Even if Congress were to use its power over the purse strings and deny the President funds for use in Cambodia or Laos or any other place, the President could still make use of funds appropriated for other purposes to carry out the ends he believes necessary—then explain his action to the people.

But Congress is not powerless. In the summer of 1970, the House Foreign Affairs Committee held hearings on House Joint Resolution 1355. It reads:

Resolved by the Senate and House of Representatives of the United States of America in Congress assembled, That the Congress reaffirms its powers under the Constitution to declare war. The Congress recognizes that the President in certain extraordinary and emergency circumstances has the authority to defend the United States and its citizens without specific prior authorization by Congress.

Sec. 2. It is the sense of Congress that whenever feasible the President should seek appropriate consultation with the Congress before involving the Armed Forces of the United States in armed conflict, and should continue such consultation periodically during such armed conflict.

Sec. 3. In any case in which the President without specific prior authorization by the Congress—

(1) commits United States military forces to armed conflict;

(2) commits military forces equipped for combat to the territory, airspace or waters of a foreign nation, except for deployment which relates solely to supply, repair, or training of United States forces, or for humanitarian or other peaceful purposes; or

(3) substantially enlarges military forces already located in a foreign nation;

the President shall submit promptly to the Speaker of the House of Representatives and to the President of the Senate a report, in writing, setting forth—

(A) the circumstances necessitating his action,

(B) the constitutional, legislative and treaty provisions under the authority of which he took such action, together with his reasons for not seeking specific prior congressional authorization;

(C) the estimated scope of activities; and

(D) such other information as the President may deem useful to the Congress in the fulfillment of its constitutional responsibilities with respect to committing the nation to war and to use of United States Armed Forces abroad.

Sec. 4. Nothing in this joint resolution is intended to alter the constitutional authority of the Congress or of the President or the provisions of existing treaties.

This resolution recognizes the practicalities. Congress can not prevent the President from using military forces abroad when he feels it is necessary. But it does compel him to report to Congress the exact nature of his actions and his reasons for them, thus offering himself and his actions to full public scrutiny. Congress could subsequently approve or denounce the action. But its most important effect would be to bring forth information that Congress and the people could use in forming public opinion. In short, the President, operating with less secrecy, would be held politically more accountable for his actions.

There is another way of restraining Presidential war powers known as "legislative oversight," the regular investigation by Congress of the conduct of national affairs. For decades Congresses have used the power of "oversight" in domestic affairs, but not in foreign affairs. The Symington subcommittee sought to alter this neglect. The subcommittee collected a great body of information and formulated policy criticisms that were useful to the President, Congress, and the people.

Many individuals and groups, including the Symington

subcommittee, have urged that Congress create permanent machinery for the investigation of foreign affairs. This would involve a full-time, permanent staff of investigators reporting directly to Congress on United States diplomatic, intelligence, military, and economic activities abroad. The President's powers would not be curbed, but he would be subjected to ongoing criticism of his policies and actions by a Congress that was informed and responsible. Secret negotiations and "creeping commitments" would be held up to public examination.

There is another curb on Presidential war powers—public opinion. A President may have a "bully pulpit" from which to rally public opinion, but that opinion does not always take the shape he desires.

There is no doubt the attention focused upon the President poses a difficulty. He and his family live a goldfish-bowl existence where minute and even intimate actions and statements are held up to public scrutiny. The President is the biggest celebrity in the world; his every action and utterance is subject to daily exposure on film or in print.

This focus of attention began with Franklin Roosevelt, who relished the attention and was a master at both encouraging and controlling it. FDR, who was a bit of a showman, staged his appearances for maximum effect. So effective was he that not until many years after his election did the majority of Americans realize he could not walk and was confined to a wheelchair. He had had polio in the prime of life.

Every President since FDR has found himself in the

goldfish bowl. The state of his health has been a national preoccupation at times. When Eisenhower had a heart attack, his consumption of food and the condition of his bowels were reported. When Lyndon Johnson had an operation, he showed the scar. Truman, angered by a critic's review of his daughter Margaret's singing, penned an irate reply that made all the newspapers. Nixon, who has the largest public relations staff of any President in history, has spent hours on television and in interviews with reporters, all in an effort to sell himself and his policies to the American people.

But Nixon, as the fifth President since FDR, has had to cope with an increasingly sophisticated and educated populace. Since 1932, the American people have witnessed constant Presidential appeals and explanations. FDR's fireside chats may have been innovative in the 1930s, but they would be old hat today. Since World War II, the United States has had one crisis after another. Presidents have made hundreds of addresses to the nation. An inevitable ennui has set in. When Nixon held a conversation with television commentator Howard Smith in April, 1971, his audience ranked a poor third behind a movie and a situation comedy.

Half the high-school graduates go to college today, and the quality of teaching at all levels is greatly improved over a generation ago. Americans know more about political techniques, as well as national and world affairs. This expertise has been aided by the press, radio, and television, for the media feel it is a duty not only to report happenings such as Presidential utterances, but to put them into context of other events and to analyze and criticize them.

Today the President is not only a molder of public opinion; he is a reactor to it. Professional pollsters permit both Presidents and the people to have some idea of public attitudes at almost any given moment. One ongoing poll offers monthly measurements of the President's popularity and of public sentiment toward his administration. Armed with (or perhaps confronted by) polls, any President feels a need to justify his actions which have met with disapproval and to take steps to maintain or improve his popularity.

Strong public antipathy to the War in Vietnam led President Johnson to halt the bombing of North Vietnam and to enter into "peace" talks. It is widely believed that public dislike for his war policies led Johnson to retire from office in 1969 when he was eligible for another term —although he has vigorously denied it.

President Nixon has reacted to public opinion many times, by withdrawing troops from Vietnam, taking television time to explain again and again his invasions of Cambodia and Laos. So great was the public outcry against the invasion of Cambodia in May, 1970, that Nixon, unable to sleep, left the White House to mingle with protestors who had converged on Washington. In 1970, he reacted to public dismay over the killing of South Vietnamese civilians by American soldiers at My Lai by calling it a "massacre."

Presidents Johnson and Nixon—and to a lesser extent their predecessors Kennedy and Eisenhower—have been afflicted with what is usually called "the credibility gap." In a word they have not been *believed*. Their versions of the facts of a happening have differed from versions provided by reporters, other officials, and foreign statesmen. An intelligent, informed American electorate is able to think for itself these days.

And the public has myriad powerful ways to express its opinion—letters, telegrams, and phone calls to the White House; petitions, protest gatherings, and demonstrations, both peaceful and violent; and finally the ballot box, where it has the option of rejecting both the President and the members of his political party.

Part II
DOMESTIC POWERS

Chapter 7
The President's
Shared Domestic
Powers

IT IS NOT POSSIBLE to separate the President's war powers from his domestic powers. Much criticism of the War in Vietnam and its extension throughout Southeast Asia resides in complaints about the incredible combination of inflation and unemployment that has occurred in the United States as a result of it. The debate over Presidential war powers is rooted in dollar facts—the United States is spending billions of dollars in its commitments abroad at a time when the nation cannot find the funds to cope with urban rot, hunger, and pollution. Our pride in sending men to the moon is diminished by the knowledge that the 400 million dollars it cost to send the Apollo 14 astronauts to that forbidding place could have been used to the most beneficial effect in New York, Chicago, Los Angeles, and other cities.

The President may a "dictator" in foreign affairs, as Senator Fulbright and many others have said, but at home he is a committeeman. He has vast powers domestically, to be sure, but in the use of them he is limited, and hedged by traditional and legal restrictions, which make the exercise of these powers a study in human cunning.

Congress may have neglected its war powers, but it most decidedly has not neglected its domestic powers. Congressmen, individually and collectively, hold great power, guard it jealously, and wield it authoritatively. There is a whole array of independent government agencies over which the President can exercise only the most nominal control and then only with the greatest difficulty. There are upwards of twenty thousand heads of government bureaus who have sufficient legal and political power to thwart the President. Washington abounds in lobbyists who, in some matters, make a mockery of Presidential domestic powers.

Only the first chapters in the tale of where the real power in Washington lies have been written. It is time that elementary books about American government were rewritten to give a more accurate picture of how things happen in the United States government and who makes them happen.

Douglass Cater's book, *Power in Washington*, was a somewhat cynical, no-holds-barred revelation of the way things happen in Washington. He referred to "subgovernments"—special, unknown combines exercising control over segments of American life. He illustrated the point with the "sugar subgovernment."

Since the early 1930s, sugar has been subject to a "cartel arrangement" sponsored by the government.

> By specific prescription [Cater writes], the sugar market is divided to the last spoonful among domestic cane and beet growers and foreign suppliers. Ostensibly to insure "stability" of supply, the U. S. price is pegged at a level considerably above the competitive price in the world market. It has been in fact a way to subsidize domestic sugar growers who are not genuinely competitive with producers abroad. For Latin American countries able to secure quotas, it has provided a bonanza of sizeable proportions.

Put in plain language, if you wish to inquire about the price stamped on a bag of sugar in the supermarkets or wonder about American commitments to sugar-producing nations of Latin America, ask the sugar "subgovernment."

It is a very small subgovernment. School books, if they mention sugar at all, would say the prices are determined by the President and Congress. In actual fact, the sugar import quotas and prices are determined by two men, the chairman of the House Agricultural Committee and the director of the Sugar Division in the Department of Agriculture. The director provides expert advice to the chairman in arranging the quotas. Further advice comes from the high-paid representatives of the domestic beet- and cane-sugar growers, the sugar refineries, and the foreign producers.

As Cater put it, the committee chairman "has the habit of receiving the interested parties one by one to make their presentations, then summoning each afterwards to announce his verdict. By all accounts, he has a zest for his princely power and enjoys the frequent meetings with foreign ambassadors to confer on matters of state and sugar."

There are scores of these "subgovernments." Some, such as sugar, are interested in only a single commodity. At the other end is the giant and celebrated "military-industrial complex." It involves thousands and thousands of key individuals, both in and outside of government, actively engaged in garnering and spending 76 billion dollars a year on national defense. Textbooks generally state that national defense is the responsibility of the President which he delegates to the Secretary of Defense. Consider the extraordinary statement of Carl Vinson, former chairman of the House Armed Services Committee:

I'd rather run the Pentagon from up here.

Professor Cater's book is a dissection of the means by which congressmen, military officers, retired officers serving industries, and an army of lobbyists and public relations men pressure Presidents, the Pentagon, and Congress for ever increasing pieces of the military pie. All may be motivated by the noble goal of military preparedness, but another result is an unseemly scramble for money, contracts, and other forms of loot.

There are many people over whom the President has no power. First among them are congressmen. They are elected by a far different constituency than the President—individual states and an assortment of miniscule districts. The powerful individuals in the House and

Senate reached those positions of power because they were elected again and again from "safe" districts where the people know they are powerful and the district or state thereby benefits. A President may rant and rail at those men, he may turn the nation against them, but he cannot remove or defeat them if their special consitituency wants them.

Much has been written about the august and awesome powers of the Presidency. In February, 1971, President Nixon proposed that Congress approve his plan for sharing federal revenues with state and local governments. He wanted the revenue to be apportioned among those governments with no strings attached. They could spend it as they wish. He considered it a bold program aimed at solving the fiscal problems of local governments.

Standing in the way of the President's plan was the formidable obstacle of Wilbur Mills, the chairman of the House Ways and Means Committee. He was opposed to the plan. He and the President met at the White House. At the President's urging, he agreed to hold full committee hearings on the plan, but added, "not for the purpose of promoting the plan—for the purpose of killing it." Mills was not being simply obstructionist. He believed the President's plan had a purely political motivation so he suggested other ways to solve the financial problems of local government short of revenue sharing.

But the President intended to fight Mills. Early in February, he held four breakfasts at the White House with Republican senators and representatives to convince them of the need for his plan. He directed cabinet members and top aides to make themselves available for television shows and to be prepared for nationwide speeches in behalf of his program. He scheduled four trips of his own to personally sell his plan to regional meetings of editors, publishers, and broadcasters. Vice President Agnew was dispatched to plead for the program with meetings of county commissioners, mayors, and other local officials. Nixon also organized twenty touring panels of three Republican Congressmen each to present his program around the country. The panelists were dubbed "Drummers for the New Revolution."

Why did the man considered to be the most powerful single individual in the world spend so much time to persuade one man, Wilbur Mills, to adopt his program? As President Truman once said:

> I sit here all day trying to persuade people to do the things they ought to have sense enough to do without my persuading them. . . . That's all the powers of the President amount to.

Second, bureaucrats. Some hold such power that the President can only wish he held so much. Many of the bureaucrats are civil servants under the merit system. They have become bureau chiefs because of ability and time on the job. Highly expert in a narrow range of affairs, they are not elected and serve under a succession of Presidents. Obviously, Presidents and policies may come and go but they will remain. Many have accumulated great power and influence among committee chairmen in Congress. Totally unknown to the public, they can with a private word or an eyebrow utterly destroy the wish of a President in a matter that falls within their province.

Early in 1971, President Nixon embarked on an economic program aimed at "spending the nation rich," that is, by increased government appropriation, by enlarging the supply of money, he hoped to reduce unemployment, to lower interest rates, to encourage individuals to spend their money rather than saving it, and thus to get the economy moving. It is painfully obvious that Mr. Nixon could not carry out that aim without congressional appropriations or fewer monetary restraints by the Federal Reserve Board. Nixon had appointed his friend Arthur Burns as chairman of that board. That body, not the President, in carrying out the responsibilities invested in it by Congress, can determine when an increase in the supply of money would be dangerously inflationary.

The power of autonomous regulatory agencies is staggering. The Federal Aviation Agency, Civil Aeronautics Board, and Interstate Commerce Commission in transportation, the Federal Trade Commission in commerce, the Securities and Exchange Commission in investment, and a host of others in matters of vital importance to the domestic affairs of the nation make a mockery of Presidential domestic power.

Incredibly, even Cabinet officers appointed by the President and serving at his discretion have legal powers that the President cannot touch. A classic example was the ability of Harold Ickes, Franklin Roosevelt's Interior Secretary, to thwart the wishes of Roosevelt and his Secretary of State to sell helium to Germany prior to World War II. Empowered by Congress to decide such a matter, Ickes refused to authorize the sale. As a result, the Germans filled their dirigibles with inflammable hydrogen gas. One airship, the *Hindenburg*, exploded with great loss of life.

Another classic example occurred in 1952 when President Truman ordered the steel industry nationalized during a threatened strike. To solve the problem, Truman developed an elaborate plan to solve the wage dispute and turn the industry back to its civilian owners. But his Commerce Secretary engaged in foot-dragging because he opposed the take-over. Truman's plan came to naught. The Supreme Court declared the seizure unconstitutional and Truman went down to an ignoble defeat.

It was perhaps with this in mind that Truman declared, after General Eisenhower was elected to succeed him:

> He'll sit here and he'll say, "Do this! Do that! *And nothing will happen*. Poor Ike—it won't be a bit like the Army. He'll find it very frustrating.

Third, lobbyists. Most Americans have either not heard of lobbyists at all or have a conception of them as corrupt individuals offering bribes along with wine, women, and song to tempt Congressmen and bureaucrats.

Such lobbyists exist, but they are an anachronism. Today's lobbyist deals in two things, friendship and expertise. He sincerely believes in what he is doing, be it in antipollution controls or a multibillion dollar contract for

an antiballistic missile. At the very least he would sub-
scribe to his own cause's or company's version of the
dictum made famous a generation ago by Charles E.
Wilson, "What is good for General Motors is good for
the nation."

Perhaps every lobbyist would deny the importance of
friendship, yet it is impossible to deny that lobbyists are
selected for their ability to use friendship. In 1959, a
House Armed Services subcommittee studied the effects
of lobbyists on the military-industrial complex. They
found that more than 1,400 retired officers of the rank
of major or higher—including 261 of general or flag rank
—were employed by the hundred biggest defense con-
tractors. One company alone employed 187 of this
group and that company was the largest single defense
contractor at the time. This study is somewhat dated as
these things go, but few would doubt that a contemporary study would reveal similar statistics.

What can retired admirals or generals do for a defense
contractor? Cater presented a devastating description of
the system. Admiral William M. Fechteler, former
Chief of Naval Operations, the Navy's highest ranking
officer, retired and went to work as a consultant for the
General Electric Co. Admiral Fechteler later described
how he arranged appointments for a visiting General
Electric vice president:

> I took him in to see Mr. Gates, the Secretary of the
> Navy. I took him in to see Admiral Arleigh Burke
> [Chief of Naval Operations]. He had not met Admiral
> Burke before. And then I made appointments with

him with the Chief of the Bureau of Ships. But I did not accompany him there, because those are materiel bureaus which make contracts. And I studiously avoid even being in the room when somebody talks about a contract.

Circumspect, certainly, but only the most naive would assume that General Electric did not consider the consultant fees paid to Admiral Fechteler to have been well earned. But even the naive would have to be influenced by the statement of Vice Admiral Hyman G. Rickover (which Cater quoted) that retired officers frequently leave their jobs to men "who are their dear friends, or . . . whom they have been influential in appointing, and naturally they will be listened to."

More than friendship, the modern lobbyist offers expertise. It has to be assumed, for example, that Admiral Fechteler, as a retired Chief of Naval Operations, was intimately aware of the problems and viewpoint of his successor, Admiral Burke, whom he visited on behalf of General Electric. He could present information which simply could not help but be useful to Admiral Burke and moreover he would have been thoroughly cognizant of the peculiar pressures and responsibilities of the Chief of Naval Operations.

Return to the sugar subgovernment. An expert lobbyist for a sugar refinery, domestic producer, or foreign sugar-exporting nation would be able to provide either the Agriculture Department bureaucrat or the chairman of the House Agriculture Committee with detailed statistics and a comprehensive analysis of the situation in the sugar business nationally and internationally that could only be useful to those individuals operating this sub-government. For you and me, knowing only how to pour sugar on a bowl of oatmeal, to duplicate those efforts is out of the question.

Congressmen and bureaucrats, wanting to use their power wisely, must rely on accurate information. The task of the lobbyist and the public relations man is to give it to him. The congressman or bureaucrat need not be approached directly. News items concerning the sugar industry, for example, can be easily placed in news-papers and on radio and television broadcasts that reveal the importance of the sugar industry or the plight of the industry in some corner of the earth. A congressman who might be turned off by a direct appeal from a lobby-ist might easily be turned on by a news item or two from his hometown newspaper.

These, then, are the ways of power in Washington: congressmen, bureaucrats, and lobbyists. In the domestic scene, and to an incredible degree in foreign affairs, this triumvirate determines what gets done in Washington and how it is performed. The President, any President, is measured by how well he controls these three forces. If he controls them well, he is effective. If he controls them poorly, he—and all Americans—are in for a time of divisiveness and dissension.

Chapter 8
Sources of
Presidential
Domestic Power

In 1960, Professor Richard E. Neustadt published a book
entitled *Presidential Power*. It was a stunning attempt
to discover *how* a President uses the powers inherent in
his office—and misuses them. President Kennedy carried
the book with him into the White House, applying many
of its principles. Neustadt became one of his advisers.

Neustadt saw Presidential influence as residing in two
distinct areas. One is the insular community of
Washington, D. C. That small town grown big is a
ferment of gossip and talk about the men who hold
power. Highly knowledegable about the sources and exercise of power in Washington, the residents of that city
operate an ongoing critique of the ability of the President
to control and use congressmen, bureaucrats, and lobbyists

who share domestic power with him. He is graded on his ability to thwart these people or to use them. If he imposes his will, he gets good marks. If they win, he gets poor marks. Good marks mean he is knowledgeable in the uses of power in Washington, that he must be listened to, and if he must not be obeyed, he cannot be disobeyed either. Consistent poor marks mean a division of power and a loss of national leadership.

The second source of influence is the power of the President with the people of the entire nation, his ability to stand before the microphones and cameras and speak directly in language people can understand, using his esteem to enlist their support. Thus, he may be able, by arousing public support, to force his program upon reluctant, power-hungry congressmen, bureaucrats, and lobbyists. At least, they will not be able to thwart him too much.

These are distinct, separate power bases. President Truman, elected as a minority President, became an increasingly unpopular President among the people. The press regularly scolded him. Opinion polls declared the people dissatisfied with him. Yet, in the Washington community, he was considered at least reasonably effective. A congressman, bureaucrat, or lobbyist who set out to thwart him felt the need to approach the matter with considerable caution. Conversely, Eisenhower throughout his two terms, and indeed to his death, remained a man loved and admired and respected by the American people. Elected by large majorities, he could count upon generally wholehearted public support for his policies. People loved him personally even when they disliked what he was doing. In Washington, however, he was considered a weak President whose power could be taken lightly. At one point a congressional committee laughed in ridicule of the President's alleged determination to force Congress to stick to his budget. Congressmen felt Eisenhower couldn't make Congress stick to anything.

Both of these sources of influence have their uses. Congress felt, in the Eisenhower administrations, that it could not openly criticize or oppose the highly popular President. Lyndon Johnson, then majority leader of the Democratic Senate, and Sam Rayburn, speaker of the Democratic House, two of the strongest men to hold those positions in recent times, both felt the need to make constant expressions of support and respect for Eisenhower. Still, Eisenhower's lack of influence in Washington enabled those two men to lead Congress in devising legislation that was more of their own making and that of their party than of Eisenhower's.

Obviously, the strongest possible President would be a man who was popular nationwide and highly regarded for his influence in Washington. Lyndon Johnson was such a man during the first two years of his term. Elected by the greatest majority in history, having swept liberal Democrats into control of the House and Senate, he led Congress into enacting one of the most far-reaching domestic programs in history, including health care for the aged, aid to education, and civil rights laws. The only other man in recent times to have had such a combination of power was Franklin Roosevelt, and he maintained it during most of his three-plus terms. Johnson's influence in Washington and particularly among the nation's people waned as the Vietnam war grew more unpopular. Kennedy, elected as a minority President in 1960 in the closest election in modern history, enjoyed relative power in Washington from the outset. By the time of his assassination, he had garnered public support. He simply did not have a chance to use the combination effectively.

President Nixon is an interesting study in the uses of these power bases as developed by Neustadt. The influence record of his first two years in office is probably best described as uneven. Elected as a minority President (44 percent of the vote) in 1968, he managed to earn widespread public support for his policies in Vietnam. He appealed to the "silent majority," as he called it, and gave evidence that he had formulated a group of suburban, Southern, and traditionally Republican supporters who would reelect him.

In Washington, his power was something else. He created a White House staff that operated as a closed society, leaving Washington bureaucrats wallowing in a state of raw fury at their loss of influence. They were not even consulted on major decisions. He persuaded Congress to enact his antiballistic missile defense system by a single vote, but later underwent a series of stunning defeats by wide margins. Two consecutive Supreme Court nominees were turned down by the Senate, a rarity in history. Two of his vetoes were overturned by both the House and Senate. His program to reform the nation's welfare system has not yet come to a vote, and his plan for revenue sharing has encountered countless problems.

After two years in office, Nixon embarked on a program to use his national popularity to force Washington into line. To an extent with few parallels, he campaigned actively in 1970 to defeat Democratic senators who had opposed him and to gain a Republican upper house. He made last-minute speeches on behalf of Republican candidates personally selected by him. He dispatched Vice President Agnew on a whirlwind campaign to elect Republicans, branding their opponents "radic-libs." The results were a loss for President Nixon, although he claimed a victory. Senator Albert Gore of Tennessee, a liberal Democrat, was narrowly defeated, and Senator Charles Goodell of New York, a liberal Republican, was replaced, as Nixon had hoped, by a Conservative. Republicans were elected in Connecticut and Ohio. But in state after state Democratic incumbents were returned to the Senate, which remained in Democratic control.

In the Neustadt concept of power, Nixon had gambled both his Washington and his national influence and lost, creating an embittered Democratic Congress eager to flex its political muscles. On the eve of the election, James Reston of *The New York Times* wrote a column entitled, "How to Lose Even if You Win."

> In a very practical sense, it is not too much or too early to say that President Nixon has already lost the election of 1970. For if the purpose of his campaign was to

make it easier for him to govern the country, it is fairly clear that his deceptive political tactics have deepened the divisions and anxieties of the people and infuriated many influential men in both parties whose support he needs to lead the nation. . . .

The President's capacity to govern has not increased but decreased and all that remains now is the judgment of the people on whether the President is to be rewarded or punished for his adventure.

Reston's prophecy of Nixon's difficulty of governing after the election is consistent with the Neustadt view of Presidential power. But, having lost, the President may still be able to govern. He switched from a preoccupation with foreign affairs to the development and launching of a domestic program. He reshuffled his cabinet and his White House Staff. He made a series of televised appearances. He began the intensive program of congressional lobbying. Election defeat or no, he set out energetically to demonstrate his capacity to govern by using the powers of his office to force his will on Congress, bureaucrats, and lobbyists.

Neustadt's provocative analysis of Presidential power showed that Presidents have power by hoarding it, by depending as little as possible on other people, by using their staff and subordinates in such a way as to gain as much information as possible from as many sources as possible, and by using power under circumstances in which they are most likely to win. Only through victory is their power enhanced. Defeat erodes power and makes for more defeat.

There are other ways of viewing Presidential power. Truman was a humble man who stood in awe of the office. Yet he was determined to keep faith with his responsibilities. He saw his duty as accepting those responsibilities, making decisions forthrightly in the nation's interests and—in language he might well use—the hell with Presidential power and popularity. Eisenhower was a so-called Whig President, who saw his job as that of uniting the country, giving a respite from aggrandizing Presidents, administering the laws, and not worrying unduly about imposing his will on Congress. Still another view was expressed by former Senator Eugene McCarthy in his campaign for the Democratic Presidential nomination in 1968. "The new politics," he said, "required a different conception of the Presidency." He saw that power not being extended in a personal way into every facet of government. He asked: "Has the integrity of Congress, of the Cabinet, and of the military been impinged upon by undue extension of the executive power?" He suggested the powers of the President be decentralized.

Most Americans tend to view the President as sitting in his oval offices issuing orders which are carried out as a sort of knee-jerk reflex of his subordinates. In contrast, consider Truman's moaning that he issued orders and nothing happened. Indeed, it is said that a President must make a "suggestion" a third time before any substantive action begins on it. If he seriously wishes it carried out, he must personally follow it with vigor or have his most trusted assistants do so.

Neustadt analyzed in great detail three Presidential orders which he termed "self-executing," President Truman's orders recalling General MacArthur as supreme commander in the Far East, his seizure of the steel industry, and President Eisenhower's dispatch of troops to Little Rock, Arkansas, during an integration crisis. Under Neustadt's analysis five common factors were at work in each instance.

> On each occasion the President's involvement was unambiguous. So were his words. His order was widely publicized. The men who received it had control of everything needed to carry it out. And they had no apparent doubt of his authority to issue it to them.

If even one of these factors was missing, Neustadt concluded, the President's orders were not self-executing. He concluded that it is extremely rare for these five factors to converge, thus enabling the President to issue a self-executing order. Neustadt felt that the three self-executing orders were a product of Presidential failure, not of success. President Truman had failed to deal with MacArthur's insubordination earlier and to force him into carrying out White House policies, and he had failed to persuade the steel industry and its labor unions to negotiate a settlement short of a strike. President Eisenhower had tried to convince Arkansas Governor Orval Faubus to agree to a court order integrating the Little Rock schools. He had failed and been left with no choice but to call out federal troops.

Neustadt's analysis is a chilling exposé of the weakness

of the President in domestic affairs. The American people elect him in the expectation that he will lead in coping with the nation's economic, social, educational, and other problems, but, faced with a powerful army of congressmen, bureaucrats, and lobbyists, he has few weapons other than persuasion. And he is caught in a situation in which, having failed to persuade, he must either use drastic powers or see his influence so eroded that he becomes ineffectual. As Truman said, "They talk about the power of the President, how I can just push a button to get things done. Why, I spend most of my time kissing somebody's ass." Or, as Lyndon Johnson said, "Power? The only power I got is nuclear—and I can't use that." Yet, both of those men will surely rank in history as "strong" Presidents who imposed their will upon the public, Congress, bureaucrats, and lobbyists.

Chapter 9
The Paradoxical
Presidential Powers

THERE is a striking contrast between the war and domestic powers of the modern President. In foreign affairs, he can develop a policy, devise the best way to carry it out, and delegate the tasks to those he pleases. After suitable conferences with his advisers, he can select from a variety of actions those which he prefers, diplomatic messages and negotiations, threats, the dispatch of ships, planes, and soldiers, or open war. Then he can explain his actions on his own terms to the people. Criticism can be ignored, at least during his term in office. He possesses abundant military, legal, and propaganda powers to accomplish what he wishes. He must cope with only very broad limitations. His responsibilities are to have a policy, make a decision, and to act. He may be thwarted by the attitudes and actions of other nations, but that is merely an invitation to further action.

In domestic affairs, the President may develop a policy and devise the best way to carry it out, but he is hamstrung all along the way in his efforts to carry it out by Congress, the bureaucracy, and the Washington lobby. He must persuade, cajole, appeal to the people, reason with those who share his power, bring political pressure on them, make deals, manipulate in an effort to get *not* what he wants, but the best he can. Defeat is frequent.

The disparity between Presidential powers abroad and at home is so great it almost seems two different men are elected to the nation's highest office.

Much of this book has focused on the debate over Presidential war powers, the belief shared by many that some sort of curbs must be placed on the President's conduct of foreign policies and his ability to engage the nation in armed conflict. There is also a debate over the Presidential domestic powers, the belief held by many that the President must be given greater authority to initiate and carry out programs to cope with the nation's problems. He must have greater power, some believe, over Congress, the bureaucracy, and the lobbyists. This debate has received far less publicity. It occurs mostly among political scientists. Members of Congress have largely ignored it. They are not eager to provide the President with more power than he already has.

Many proposals for increasing the Presidential domestic powers have been made, but three are paramount. The first would repeal the Twenty-second Amendment to the

Constitution, which restricts a President to two terms. It was proposed by the Republican Eightieth Congress after World War II in an act of spite against Franklin Roosevelt, who served three terms and part of a fourth (but it did not apply to Harry S Truman who was President at the time the amendment was ratified in 1951.) The two-term tradition had started with George Washington and continued until 1940 when Roosevelt broke it. Back in power in 1947, the Republicans pushed through the amendment forbidding third terms and it was quickly ratified by the state legislatures.

The arguments in favor of the amendment are that it honors the tradition set by Washington. It makes a dictatorship much more difficult in the United States. Finally, it permits the President to be above politics during his second term. Forbidden to run again, he is freed from the need to play politics and thus, theoretically, can act wisely in the nation's interests.

Those who urge repeal of the amendment argue that it is not possible to accomplish very much in the United States government without politics. And in his second term, the President lacks the sort of political muscle derived from knowledge that he might run again. By keeping Congress and the people guessing, he can apply pressure to those who share his power. Political scientists feel that there was a distinct drop in the effectiveness of Eisenhower when he could not seek another term.

The second proposal is to give the President a *line veto* over appropriations. At present, the President must either accept an entire bill or reject it *in toto*, and it is virtually impossible for him to do the latter. The government has to operate. Employees must be paid. Chaos would result if the Department of Defense, say, had its appropriations bill vetoed by the President.

Knowing this, Congress often attaches amendments or "riders" to appropriations. These riders may be entirely unrelated to the subject of the main legislation and they are frequently something the President does not want. Late in 1970, Congress sought to attach a highly controversial tariff bill as an amendment to the Social Security bill. Higher benefits for Social Security recipients were highly desired by everyone, including President Nixon, but many people objected to higher tariffs, including President Nixon. If the bill had passed, the President would either have had to accept tariffs to get more aid for the elderly, widowed, and orphaned—or been in the position of vetoing such benefits to prevent the nation from launching an international tariff war.

Congress passes scores of such riders every session. Many are of the log-rolling variety, spending money for federal installations in the states and districts of powerful congressmen. The President must generally accept them. With the line veto, which some state governors have, the President could accept the bill, but veto one or more portions of it. Thus, he could have vetoed the tariff, while accepting the higher Social Security benefits.

Some political scientists believe the line veto would give the President too much power over Congress. Others feel he needs it. Perhaps the most sensible suggestion was made by Professor Rossiter. He suggested that the line veto be tried for a short period of time in one specific area of appropriations as an experiment to assess its effects.

The third proposal, which is now before Congress and the nation for consideration and debate, calls for a drastic reorganization of the executive branch to give the President greater control over the bureaucracy.

In his State of the Union message in January, 1971, President Nixon suggested that seven cabinet-level departments be abolished and formed into four superdepartments, each headed by a man appointed by the President and approved by the Senate. This is an attempt to centralize authority, reduce the number of men in whom the President must invest power, and simplify his tasks.

The second proposal comes from a study by a Presidential commission headed by businessman Roy Ash. The commission recommended that nearly all the federal regulatory agencies be abolished in their present form and be reconstituted in a new form each headed by a single individual serving at the pleasure of the President.

At present, the regulatory commissions—such as the Interstate Commerce Commission, Federal Trade Commission, Federal Power Commission, Securities and Exchange Commisison, Federal Communications Commission, and many others—were set up as quasi-independent agencies headed by a commission. The President appoints the commissioners, but their term is not coincident with his and he cannot replace them or exert more than nominal control over them. The intention of Congress was that these agencies be independent of political persuasion and more free to act in the nation's interest. In actual fact, the agencies, grown powerful, exercise independent judgment for good or ill without any real control by the President or Congress.

The Ash Commission suggested abolishing all but one of the agencies and combining them in various ways. The single administrators of the then smaller number of agencies would be directly responsible to the President, as cabinet officers are now. (The exception was the Federal Communications Commission, which it was argued needs to reflect the various point of view of the sensitive broadcasting industry.)

Both of these reorganization proposals are certain to be hotly debated in Congress. Passage is expected to take several years—if it occurs at all—for the effect of the plans will be to lessen the power of Congress and the bureaucracy, while enhancing the President's.

What sort of man would be most effective in carrying out the powers granted to the President of the United States? In domestic affairs, a President to be effective must be strong, willful, and persuasive. He must be able to appeal to a sufficiently large majority of Americans so as to garner their overwhelming support. In the White House, he must be strong and knowledgeable enough to show the Washington community that he knows what he wants, has the determination to see it through, and can get it done. He must be able to badger, threaten, or otherwise influence congressmen, both from his own party and the opposition. He must know how to make them use their power to meet his ends. He must be able to force bureaucrats to support him and to use lobbyists for his own ends.

By any standard, the job calls for an extraordinary man, and the American people have elected a number of them.

But what of the man using his war powers? He needs to be decisive and dynamic, but he has relatively less need to persuade and manipulate, certainly in a situation of crisis. His problem is to decide what is best and to carry it out. But so great is the military power of the United States, so great is its responsibility in a nuclear age, his principal problem is often an exercise in restraint. A civil war in Asia, an insurgency in South America, a Communist plot in Africa, a financial crisis in Europe, a downed American plane, a captured ship—all and a dozen more can provoke a President to decisive action using the military force at his exclusive command.

In short, Americans are looking for a strong, willful man in domestic affairs and a strong, restrained man in foreign matters. It is surely an unusual combination to ask a man to be powerful where his strength is limited and to be limited where his strength is powerful. But an unusual combination or not, that is probably what most Americans seek in their President.

Starting in 1972, Americans aged 18, 19, and 20 will be permitted to vote for President for the first time in history. In my opinion, the authorizing legislation was adopted by Congress and signed by President Nixon as a conscious effort to involve young people, many of whom are in dissent against the nation's policies and attitudes, in the electoral process.

That process involves understanding those paradoxical powers of the Presidency and then demanding that the candidates express how they will exercise those powers and, finally, selecting the man most likely to exercise them well.

This may not be easy for an individual voter, but among Americans there is a collective wisdom. It has been demonstrated at the polls hundreds of times, with voters refusing to be stampeded, bought, or bamboozled by clever political tricks. No one should know the power of public opinion better than the American teen-ager. For the last decade he (and his older brothers and sisters) have through protests, demonstrations, and some violence, made national issues out of civil rights and racial equality, the Vietnamese war, and ecology. In fact, public opinion germinating among young people has led the nation into a reexamination of its institutions, morality, and priorities.

With many people questioning both the war and domestic powers of the Presidency, there is good reason to believe that many Americans are thinking about these problems and searching for solutions. Thus, no voter in casting his opinion by ballot is quite alone. Participation in the electoral process is valuable. I hope you will participate.

Bibliography

This is not intended as an exhaustive list of all the sources used in this book, but rather as a list of the most accessible, those of greatest interest to me and to the reader wishing to pursue the subject.

BOOKS

Bowen, Catherine Drinker. *Miracle at Philadelphia*. Little Brown, New York, 1966.

Burns, James MacGregor. *Roosevelt: The Soldier of Freedom*. Harcourt, Brace & World, New York, 1970.

Cater, Douglass. *Power in Washington*. Alfred A. Knopf, New York, 1964.

Eisenhower, Dwight D. *Waging Peace, 1956–1961*. Doubleday & Co., New York, 1965.

Goldman, Eric F. *The Tragedy of Lyndon Johnson.* Alfred A. Knopf, New York, 1968.

Laski, Harold J. *The American Presidency.* Harper & Brothers, New York, 1940.

Neustadt, Richard E. *Presidential Power: The Politics of Leadership.* John Wiley & Sons, New York, 1960.

Phillips, Cabell. *The Truman Presidency.* Macmillan, New York, 1966.

Rossiter, Clinton. *The American Presidency.* Harcourt, Brace & World, New York, 1956, 1960.

Sorensen, Theodore C. *Kennedy.* Harper & Row, New York, 1965.

Taft, William Howard. *The President and His Powers.* Columbia University Press, New York, 1916.

Walton, Richard J. *Beyond Diplomacy.* Parents' Magazine Press, New York, 1970.

Warren, Sidney. *The President as World Leader.* J. B. Lippincott, Philadelphia, 1964.

ARTICLES

Bresler, Robert J., "The War-Making Machinery," *Nation*, Aug. 17, 1970.

Coffin, Tristram, "Congress: It's Lost Sacred Powers," *Bulletin of the Atomic Scientists*, Dec. 1967.

Commager, Henry Steele, "Can We Limit Presidential Power?," *New Republic*, Apr. 6, 1968.

Cunliffe, Marcus, "A Defective Institution?," *Commentary*, Feb. 1968.

Cousins, Norman, "The Four Centers of U. S. Foreign Policy," *Saturday Review*, July 2, 1966.

Felix, Christopher, "The Unknowable CIA," *Reporter*, Apr. 6, 1968.

Morganthau, Hans J., "Who Makes Those Commitments? Congress and Foreign Policy," *New Republic*, June 14, 1969.

Padover, Saul K., "The Power of the President," *Commonweal*, Aug. 9, 1968.

Pusey, Merlo J., "The President and the Power to Make War," *Atlantic Monthly*, July, 1969.

Schlesinger, Arthur, Jr., "The Limits and Excesses of Presidential Power," *Saturday Review*, May 3, 1969.

Wicker, Tom, "The Presidency Under Scrutiny," *Harper's*, Oct. 1969.

(The excellent series of seven articles on American foreign policy which *The New York Times* published in January, 1971, is available in pamphlet form. Write Public Relations Department, The New York Times, New York, N. Y. 10036. Enclose $1.)

GOVERNMENT PUBLICATIONS

Senate Foreign Relations Committee:
Foreign Military Sales Act Amendments: 1970, 1971
Arms Control and Disarmament Act Amendments, 1970
United States Recognition of Foreign Governments
Security Agreements and Commitments Abroad. (Symington Subcommittee)
Background Information on the Use of United States Armed Forces in Foreign Countries

Index

About the Author

ROBERT A. LISTON has a score of writing credits. Mr. Liston was born in Youngstown, Ohio. He graduated from Hiram College, Hiram, Ohio with a major in history and political science. Mr. Liston has written for newspapers and magazines. He now devotes most of his time to writing books for young people. School Library Journal selected his book, DOWNTOWN: Our Challenging Urban Problems (Delacorte Press) as one of the best books for young people published in 1968. For McGraw-Hill he has written, GREETING: YOU ARE HEREBY INDUCTED . . . The Draft in America; DISSENT IN AMERICA; SLAVERY IN AMERICA: The History of Slavery; and SLAVERY IN AMERICA: The Heritage of Slavery.